CINCINNATI'S
MUSIC HALL

JORDAN & COMPANY
VIRGINIA BEACH

CINCINNATI'S
MUSIC HALL

WITH ESSAYS BY ZANE L. MILLER AND
GEORGE F. ROTH A. I. A.
AND AN INTRODUCTION BY LUKE FECK

DESIGNED BY L. BARRY MOORE
PHOTOGRAPHY BY SANDY UNDERWOOD

Library of Congress Catalogue Number 78-54665
ISBN 0-918908-04-3.

Jordan & Company, Publishers Inc.
1213 Laskin Rd., Suite 205
Virginia Beach, Virginia 23451

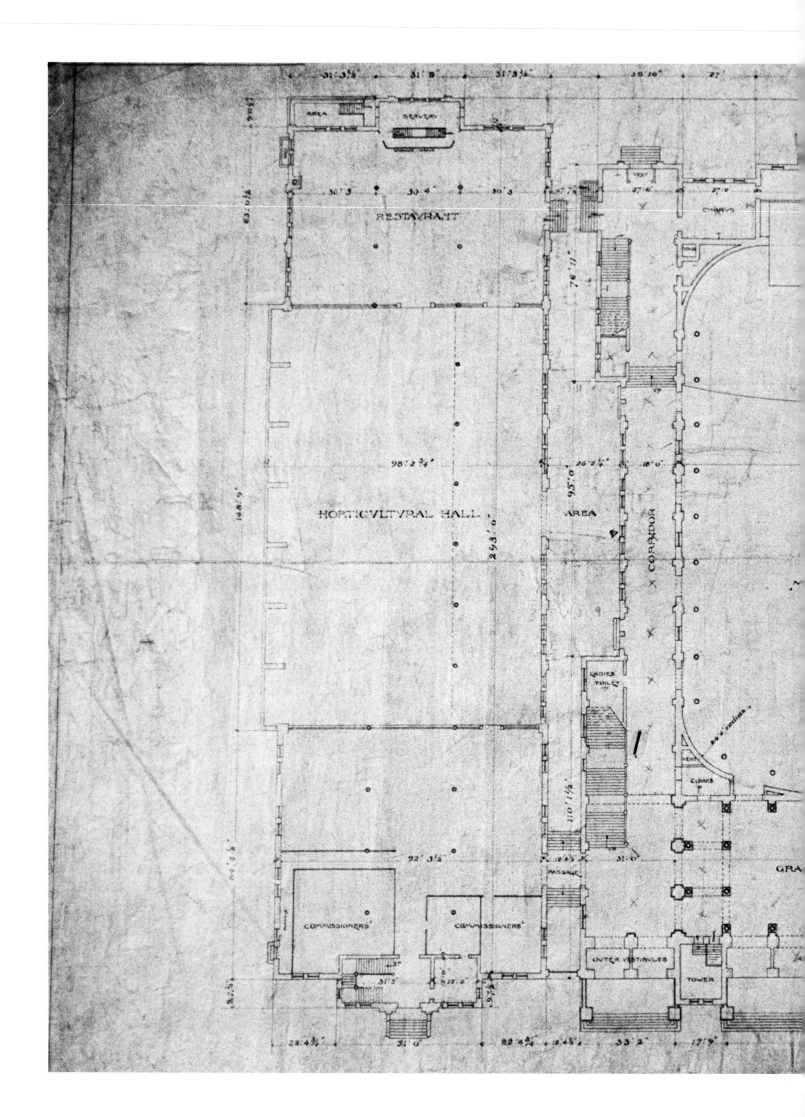

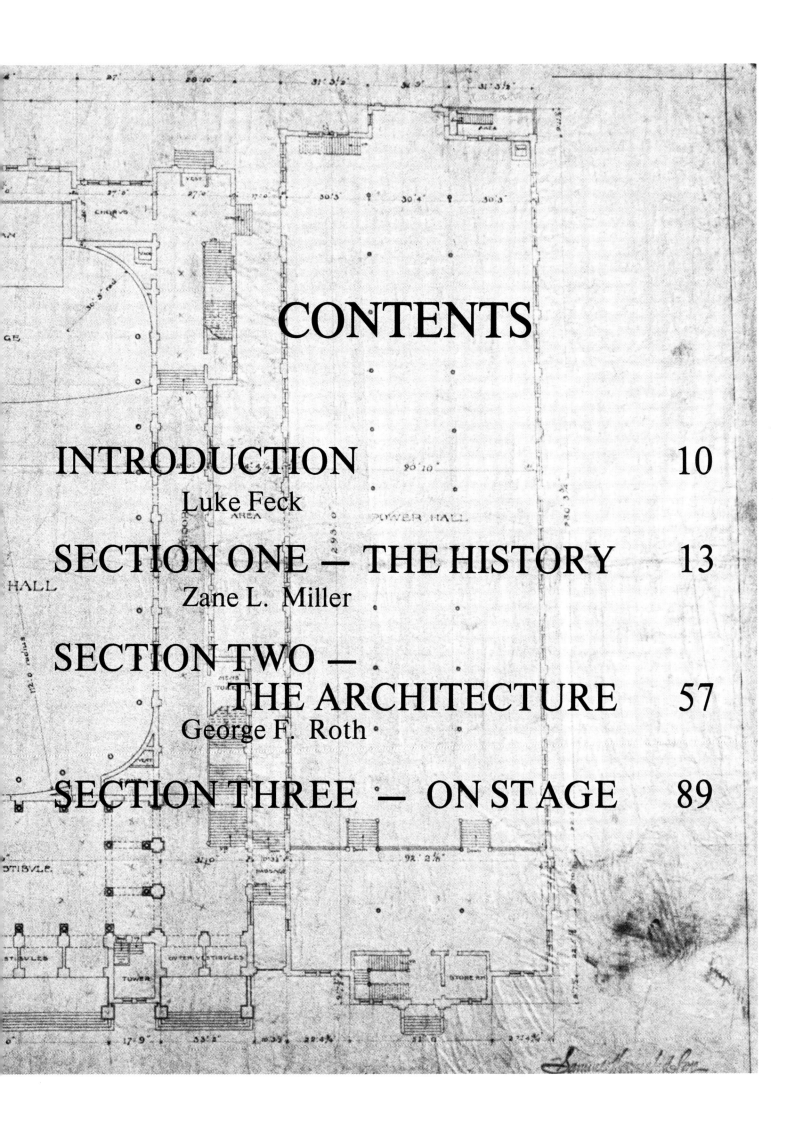

CONTENTS

Dedication

*In gratitude to J. Ralph and Patricia Corbett
and to the people of Cincinnati.*

Introduction

Reuben R. Springer called it Cincinnati Music Hall. Technically, it is Springer Hall. But really it's just plain Music Hall, isn't it?

Cincinnati embraces its institutions — and Music Hall is one — with love, with care but always slowly, gradually. It takes time to earn a spot close to the Queen City's maternal heart. Time and mutual respect are the key. Cincinnati's basic institutions are each more than 100 years old and each has won its place through years of utility and reliability — like a favorite sweater worn against the chill.

It doesn't make any difference that the Suspension Bridge is blue. That bridge beat back the ravaging flood of 1937 and kept a way open between Kentucky and Ohio when the rest of the river was closed down. It isn't color or hue that counts. Power and might buried in a fine aesthetic arc make the bridge one of the city's symbols. It doesn't matter that pigeons roosted on the regal brow of the Tyler Davidson Memorial Fountain. They soiled her and stained her but she stood up through it all, to serve as a symbol of a re-awakened center city. It didn't matter that the Reds languished in baseball's nether regions for so many years. They are, after all, a singularity in Greater Cincinnati, perhaps in America. When they began to perform as the fans knew they should/could, the Reds were enshrined again as the institution named simply "our Reds."

This book is about another Cincinnati institution, Music Hall. Some describe it as an architectural eccentric, others as sauerbraten Byzantine and others merely busy. Some call it Italianesque Gothic or high Victorian but poets see it as "the voice of the people speaking in their building." When the building was designed, those voices were singing.

It was music, rain and tin that prompted Reuben R. Springer to help give Cincinnati her Music Hall.

The second half of opening night of the May Festival of 1875 was about to begin. Torrential rains danced on the tin roof of Music Hall's predecessor, Saengerfest Hall. The din deafened and lasted for more than a half an hour before Maestro Theodore Thomas would begin again. Because of the noise, Springer felt we should have a hall to properly house a growing musical tradition.

Dr. Zane L. Miller, professor of history at the University of Cincinnati, has carefully documented the history and sociological impact of Music Hall in a more scholarly fashion than this historical anecdote. George F. Roth, architect and former professor of history of architecture at the University of Cincinnati, provides a definitive account of the design and building of Music Hall. Sandy Underwood, a talented photographer active in photography of the arts, has provided a collection of pictures capturing the intensity and joy of Music Hall for entertainer and audience alike.

Though we think of music when we think of Music Hall, there were battle lines formed by the music forces and the exposition forces, as Dr. Miller explains. It was fortunate. The building became central in the city's affairs. In 1880,

Luke Feck

10

the Democratic National Convention nominated Winfield Scott Hancock for the presidency at Music Hall. An elaborate memorial service was held there for Salmon P. Chase, chief justice of the United States. Some three thousand sat down to a sumptuous banquet in Music Hall to celebrate the completion of the city's own Southern Railroad. The Court House Riot of 1884 started as an orderly protest meeting at Music Hall. A massive memorial service was sung at Music Hall in 1884 in memory of the victims of that year's flood. The first educational TV station in America, WCET, was born at Music Hall. The Technical School of Cincinnati, which later became the University of Cincinnati College of Engineering, started in Music Hall. The Cincinnati College of Music began in Music Hall. William Jennings Bryant spoke there, Billy Sunday preached there, Buster Crabbe swam there, Gorgeous George wrestled there, and thousands of corsaged teen-aged girls went to proms there.

During one topsy-turvy period, the Topper Club earned more income for the Music Hall complex than did the hall itself. The Topper, in the South Wing, was part and parcel of the post-pubescent period for most Cincinnati youngsters. A huge sphinx embraced orchestras playing at the Topper. Frequently, it transformed typical students into prom queens, honorary cadet colonels, Sophos queens or kampus kings. The strains of "Good Night Sweetheart" serenaded the young and kept the venerable hall in some semblance of shape until help arrived.

And help was needed. The hall endured and flourished after several major refurbishings, but by the middle 1960's Music Hall was in trouble. There was even talk, back then, of tearing the hall down. Just as there would have been no Music Hall without Reuben Springer, there would be no Music Hall without Ralph and Patricia Corbett.

Commitment characterizes Cincinnati philanthropy. Music Hall cost $496,943.78 and Springer contributed almost half the amount. Beginning in 1969, and concluding in 1975, the Corbett Foundation spent almost $6 million of the $10.5 million needed to renovate the hall and develop parking space.

Planning and care went into the commitment to restore Music Hall. The Corbetts talked with ushers and patrons, ticket takers and administrators before their foundation grants were made. Since opera was to be sung in summer, the huge hall needed air-conditioning. Cooling, rushing air makes noise that might interfere with the hall's splendid acoustics so baffles were built into the ductwork to keep the air quiet, if not still.

Seating had deteriorated. Girth is greater today than it was 100 years ago. Legs are longer. Sightlines were not as good as they should have been. The 3632-seat auditorium was redone from the flooring up for the audiences of today. Long-lasting mohair seats were ordered. Aisles were recarpeted. Seats to the rear were raised several feet for unobstructed vision. Box seats were refurnished. That renovation project alone cost $451,780.

While millions were spent in public areas, a similar amount went backstage and into administrative areas. The North Wing, where the University of Cincinnati once played basketball and show horses cavorted, was gutted. Opera scenery could be stored there. The first floor of the South Wing was remodeled into needed administrative offices for the musical arts — symphony, opera, May Festival and ballet.

Now, in its Centennial year, Music Hall is a restored gem in the Queen City's crown, its sandblasted brick at Central Parkway glowing in the beams of the setting sun.

In May of 1975, a letter was sent to Ralph and Patricia Corbett. It said: "I read with interest and some sorrow the story in Wednesday morning's paper about the winding down of your foundation . . . The city was lucky when Powel Crosley first brought you here. Your benefactions are impressive. The restoration of Music Hall was monumental. As a Cincinnatian who feels privileged to have met you, I would just like to say, simply, thank you. The lives of my children and their children will be enriched because of the Corbetts."

A hand-written note was received in reply: "In all frankness, I was deeply touched by your note. As the foundation approaches its wind-up, I find myself getting moody, restless and somewhat morose.

"I came to Cincinnati in the early 1930s — after two devastating setbacks in New York — the aftermath of the big stock market crash (which wiped me out). The other happening was my decision to avoid the practice of law — something I had planned for with great eagerness.

"It was Powel Crosley of WLW who invited me here — as a consultant to the station. After several years I was able to 'rebuild' my career and finances. I built a house on an 80-acre farm property — raised my two children there. The rest is well known — I built a company which prospered (not without many heartaches) — and vowed that some day I would repay Cincinnati for the good things which happened to me.

"There it is — now it is coming to an end — and I feel deeply sad. And yet I am comforted by the record of accomplishments of our Foundation — and what my wife and I were able to do in this city for the arts, for medical and educational projects. — Ralph"

As Music Hall begins its second 100 years of service, we have been showered with a great good fortune. Within the ranks of our people we have always found enough care and commitment to get the job done — and not just done. Well done. We had a Roebling for our bridge, a Probasco for our fountain, a Springer and the Corbetts for our Music Hall.

Perhaps this tradition of citizen commitment and participation is Cincinnati's finest institution of all.

Luke Feck
Cincinnati, Ohio
April, 1978

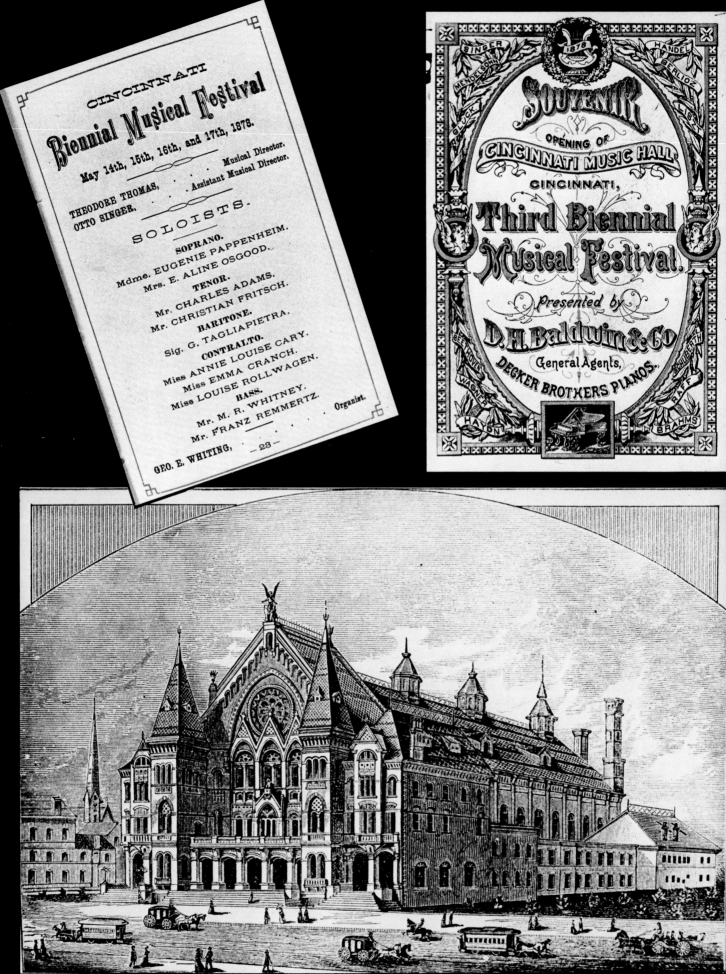

SECTION ONE
THE HISTORY

Introduction

Dr. Neil Harris

The worlds of poetry and power, which Robert Frost described for a presidential inaugural 18 years ago, have never been insulated from one another in America. But Zane Miller's essay reveals just how many ties link an institution committed to artistic expression and the changing life of its host city. It is clear that the Cincinnati Music Hall depended not only on the good will and encouragement of local patrons and municipal government, but that its health, site, and varying functions were tied to the shifting status of Cincinnati itself.

We have begun, in the 1970s, to witness the centennials of a remarkable number of major cultural institutions. Museums, libraries, symphonies, and opera companies have birthdays which suggest that more than mere coincidence was involved in the flowering of urban culture that occurred in the 1870s and 1880s. Specific patterns varied, and what happened in Cincinnati or Chicago differed from events in Denver and Boston. But there was sharing, a sharing which was a response to two powerful American images: the vision of the Ideal City, and the dream of the Virtuous Countryside. In the late 19th century, under the strain of rapid urbanization, both images exerted powerful appeal.

City government, according to foreign observers, was the single failure of American democracy. Cities were perceived, even by some of their most respectable residents, as concentrations of poverty, deviance, eroticism, and squalor.

Despite these attacks, some saw the American city as a new kind of frontier, a special test for American democracy, a crucible in which the races of mankind would be mingled and melted down to form the American Type. Aided by the favored possessors of wealth and cultivation, and by a cleansed and efficient municipal government, American cities could yet achieve miracles of beauty and technology. The expositions of the late part of the century dramatized the possibilities of urban planning, and were called Dream Cities, White Cities, Ivory Cities, to suggest their brilliant achievements.

The urban culture developed then, as Professor Miller points out, with a missionary zeal; the hoped-for conversion was multiple. On the one hand, the unlettered and unwashed would be refined by the cleansing power of great art and music. And on the other, municipal reputations, suffering from rural assault and foreign ridicule, would be redeemed by association with these grand aims.

It is normal to assume that neither of these objectives was ever attained. The urban masses had their own cultures, filled with rituals, music, craft arts, and literatures that explicated their own life patterns. The museums and symphonies were distant institutions which had little effect upon their values or behavior.

And yet conventional criticism may be somewhat misdirected. For civic cultural institutions have had a great deal to do with shaping local identity and achieving wider distinction. This was particularly true in the late 19th century, when so much cultural activity had a special aim: the demonstration of a newly-attained margin, a surplus, an amplitude that was the product of industrialization and population growth. For too long attention had been lavished, Americans argued, on the provision of essential services; it was now necessary to move beyond them.

In the early 19th century, cultural nationalists had approached the problem from the creator's point of view. National genius was demonstrated by the presence of poets, painters, writers, sculptors, and architects. But in the late 19th century, the consumer's view took on greater importance. Whether or not we composed our own music, we could create more opportunities for listening to it. In a way, a city's reputation was probably enhanced more by its theatres, museums, and concert halls than by the living presence of an artistic community. For while creative artists demonstrated local talent, cultural institutions were proof of cultural taste. And taste was so desired because it signaled that judgment followed wealth.

The cultural institutions of the late 19th century, moreover, were more tolerant and latitudinarian than they are often depicted. It was no sin, in Chicago, to mingle business conventions, a hotel, and a concert hall in the great Auditorium. It was not demeaning for the Art Institute to host exhibitions of children's art and send some of its collection on expeditions throughout the city. When local pride, nationalism, and consumer pleasure were added to the staples of high culture, the result was a blend in which grand opera and melodrama, or photography and history painting, might be close neighbors.

Cultural consumption, in the late 19th century metropolis, could provide a basis for a community more enduring than the accidents of geography and economic motive.

For conservatives it demonstrated that higher ideals co-existed with mercenary motives. For immigrants, it meant a reassertion of the high cultures of their mother countries, and sometimes an opportunity to demonstrate how craft gifts carried across the ocean could be made applicable to the conditions of American life. And to reformers, art consumption was a hostage to fortune, a sign that utopian visions of community might yet be attained.

This vision of urbanity has met many challenges in the 20th century, ideological as well as economic. In certain cities it was distorted by the vast movements of energy and resources, which Professor Miller describes. But it

These three photographs, taken in 1875, show an excellent panoramic view of the basin and convey a sense of the compactness of the "walking city."

vertical movement restricted to pedestrian proportions, even the most populace places remained compact entities of mixed land and building uses and squat skylines of three and four story buildings pierced only by church spires. Institutional structures characteristically provided quarters for multiple and disparate activities, and the boarding house, hotel, and tenement constituted the city's predominant residential housing types. This kind of urban milieu rendered the word "neighborhood" meaningless, except as a phrase indicating simple geographic proximity, and it blurred the boundries and diversified the functions of downtown. It also placed a high premium on sites close to the river, waterfront, or railway terminals, the chief points of entry to any mid-19th century big city. But because of its inaccessibility, real estate on the urban periphery was relatively cheap, leaving those areas of the city to serve as the typical locale of the greenest immigrants, the poor, blacks, and criminal elements, and virtually the only conceivable location for any large, land-intensive institution. As a consequence, hospitals, cemeteries, workhouses, markets, factories, slaughterhouses, and railroads occupied scattered locations on the margins of town noteworthy for their lack of centrality, scruffiness, and reputation for dirt, disorder and disease.

Cincinnati in 1870 matched almost perfectly this model of the mid-19th century "walking city." Though its population then stood at 216,239, the bulk of its people, commerce and industry remained confined to the basin between the river and the surrounding networks of hills. The riverfront flats below Fourth Street contained a jumble of warehouses, factories, hotels, small tenements, and cheap lodging houses. The central business district comprised a tight rectangle bounded by Third and Sixth and Central and Broadway. Railway terminals and factories crowded among residences in the East End, the Deer Creek bottoms along what is now Eggleston Avenue, and the lower West End from the Ohio River up Mill Creek Valley to Eighth Street. Factories, slaughterhouses and a diversity of other businesses fell in an arc stretching from the Mohawk-Brighton district at the foot of Clifton hill along the Miami and Erie Canal (now Central Parkway) to its eastern terminus just above the slums of Bucktown, the city's largest single black

enclave, and the factories in the lower reaches of Deer Creek Valley.

Between the canal and the hills on the northern edge of the basin lay the Over-the-Rhine district, a peripheral region of the city whose residential population included a high proportion of recently arrived Germans, and whose southern boundry had been the scene of anti-Catholic and nativistic political rioting in the 1850s. It also contained Findlay Market, and a burying grounds on 12th street between Race and Elm converted by the city in the 1850s into Washington Park. Just to the park's west, inside the elbow created by the northerly swing of the Canal, lay three and one-half acres known as the Orphan Asylum plot, and west of it beyond the canal sat the Commercial Hospital, which two decades before occupied land closer to the Ohio River. Horsedrawn street railways installed in the 1860s and running generally from what is now Fountain Square to Mohawk-Brighton and beyond toward Mill Creek Valley, the next most likely region of rapid urban growth, comprised the only regular means of public transit, other than horse pulled carts, carriages, and omnibuses, the only non-pedestrian method of moving people and things across this compact, volatile and undifferentiated territorial assemblage of humans and their institutions.

Given Cincinnati's "walking city" geography, finding a suitable site for a grand exposition posed a formidable challenge. The event would presumably attract from all points of the compass large numbers of visitors, exhibitors, and their products. Guests would require lodgings, and the ground would not only have to be large enough to accommodate a diverse array of exhibits but be accessible to the entry points through which the crowds and exhibits themselves would arrive. Clearly, because of space requirements, the location would have to be on the periphery of the city, a desideratum which, given the poverty, disorderliness and squalor of that region, made difficult the task of providing visitors with a sense of security and a favorable impression of the beauty, prosperity, progress, health and comfort of Cincinnati. Yet finding a site took little time, for by virtue of a complicated series of mid-19th century real estate exchanges the city in 1870 owned the three and one-half acre Orphan Asylum plot across from Washington Park on Elm Street above Twelfth.

Originally the location of a branch of the Commercial Hospital called the Pest House because of its use for the incarceration of persons with contagious diseases, the tract came in the 1830s into the possession of the managers of the Cincinnati Orphan Asylum. Cincinnati annexed the area above the canal in 1849. Then, in the 1850s the Asylum managers purchased property on Mt. Auburn and sold its Elm street holdings to the city for $150,000 to provide more space for Commercial Hospital. During the 1850s the city also obtained control of the land across the street from the Orphan Asylum which ultimately because Washington Park, but which Council originally planned to use as the new site for the hospital. That scheme fell through, however, and in the 1860s the city sold bonds to finance the tearing down and

"Mt. Auburn, Corryville & Avondale" coach lines served the hilltop residents of Cincinnati in 1870. (Gilbert Eversull)

Surrounding hills and limited public transportation made Cincinnati a "walking city" in the-1800s. A network of horse-car lines ultimately cover the downtown area, up the Millcreek Valley and to the East End. Few dared the hillsides like this Mt. Auburn, Corryville & Avondale coach of 1870.

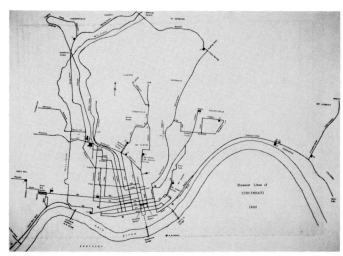

A map of the horsecar lines in 1880.

reconstruction of Commercial Hospital, by now called Cincinnati Hospital, on its old site west of the canal, on Twelfth Street between Plum Street and Central Avenue. During construction, the hospital moved into temporary quarters, one of which was the old Asylum on Elm above Twelfth between the canal and Washington Park.

Completion of the new hospital in 1869 vacated the temporary "Elm Street Branch on the Orphan Asylum plot," which the city made available to the Nord-Amerikanisches Saengerbund, an international singing society with headquarters in Cincinnati which planned to hold its 1870 convention in Cincinnati. The General Committee of the exposition secured temporary use of the property by agreeing to put up $5000 for the hasty

construction of a large wooden hall for the Saengerfest, designing the building in such a way that it would be suitable for the 1870 exposition after the termination of the Saengerfest.

The old Orphan Asylum site proved attractive to the exposition organizers for several reasons. Its location on the canal made it accessible by boat and it lay on a major south-north street almost directly north of the new Grand Hotel and of the terminals of railroads entering the city through the Millcreek Valley. The horse-drawn street railway system tied the site both to downtown hotels and the fashionable residential district, railway terminals, and factories in the east end. In addition, the site possessed protection from the surrounding neighborhood, for it was

Although railroads were creeping in, steamboats still played a major part in Cincinnati's transportation picture until late in the century, as indicated by this engraving of Cincinnati not long after the post-Civil War completion of the Suspension Bridge.

CINCINNATI HOSPITAL — FRONT VIEW

Thousands of concert-goers parked their cars on "the old hospital lot" across Central Parkway from Music Hall over the years. This was the Cincinnati Hospital that stood across the canal from the Music Hall site, originally acquired by the city to provide room for hospital expansion.

buffered to the south by the canal, to the west by the canal and the Cincinnati Hospital, and to the east by Washington Park. It was, moreover, free and, by mid-19th century walking city standards, luxuriously spacious.

When completely developed for the 1870 exposition, the ground contained not only the Main Hall originally projected, but three others: Power Hall, a novel feature of the exposition which displayed the inner-workings of steam-age factory machines; a Fine Arts and Music Hall divided into four long apartments; and a Mechanics Hall to showcase the skill and inventive ingenuity of works in the manual arts. At later expositions in the 1870s the General Committee also put up a Horticulture Hall for the exhibition of landscape techniques for beautifying suburban estates, parks, and cemeteries, and added a separate Art Hall in Washington Park connected to the other buildings by a pedestrian bridge across Elm Street.

By the mid-1870s, in short, the General Committee had put together in a park setting accommodations for expositions designed to edify, uplift, and educate their viewers and to impress visitors with the progress of civilization in the broad region which their promoters hoped would be dominated by Cincinnati, the Queen City of the West, the heart and center of the American republic. Only one flaw marred the site. It was a temporary location, controlled by the city.

The resolution of that problem took several years to accomplish, during which time the exposition took place on the old Orphan Asylum grounds, and the final solution broadened the function of the exposition site, while remaining true to the spirit which created it, and led to the construction of Music Hall.

The movement began when Maria Longworth Nichols, the daughter of Joseph Longworth, who had accumulated a vast fortune in real estate speculation in and around Cincinnati, and the wife of George Ward Nichols, who had studied painting in France and served as art critic for the *New York Evening Post* before moving to the Queen City in 1868 to marry Miss Longworth, conceived the idea of holding in Cincinnati a music festival. She wanted it, like the famous festival in Birmingham, England, to feature the performance of both choral and orchestral masterworks. Her husband, who liked to couple descriptions "of the extent and character of Cincinnati's manufactures . . . with an elaborate argument upon the necessity and utility of art in advancing and varying them by means of general art culture," organized a committee to handle the business details, including the establishment of a $30,000 guarantee fund. Then, in a bid for national recognition, Maria Nichols persuaded Theodore Thomas, the conductor of a New York based symphony orchestra which held concerts in Central Park and which since 1869 had made annual tours of major cities of the east and west, including Cincinnati, to act as its musical director.[4]

Under these auspices the first Cincinnati Musical Festival took place in 1873 in the Music Hall, sometimes called Saengerfest Hall, on the Exposition grounds. Its object was to provide in Cincinnati exhibits of musical culture on a higher artistic plane than those associated with the essentially social and convivial demonstrations of the Saengerfest — a goal which prompted the *Cincinnati Volksfreund* to criticize the Musical Festival as "too serious" an event whose "present audience consists

mostly of the money aristocracy of the Queen City" — and to bring to the city the choral societies of America, and especially the west. The initial Festival attracted thirty-six societies from places as distant as Des Moines, Iowa, and Titusville, Pennsylvania, and proved so successful that its organizers incorporated the Musical Festival Association to make the occasion a permanent feature of Cincinnati life. But from the beginning some of its supporters sought a larger aim. As the *Cincinnati Commercial* put it, "There has been glory in it, and, unexpectedly, money also." Why not, the editor asked, construct a grand hall as a site for the festival? "With such a Hall," he argued, "Cincinnati, the center of the Nation as to population would be not only the music and art capital, but the City of National Conventions, political and religious."

Construction of a hall of such grandiose proportions raised once more the issue of a site and the question of collecting a large sum of money, much more than the $25,000 and $30,000 gathered by the associations launched the exposition movement. And though conceivable in the mid-19th century that the municipality might lend its credit to a transportation venture, like the Southern railroad, or for an institution as obviously related to the health of the city as the Cincinnati Hospital, civic agencies for moral, aesthetic and educational uplift characteristically stemmed from groups of individuals acting under corporate charter or some other legal mandate from the state and managed by a board of commission dominated by the incorporators or association members. The erection of common schools in the 1820s helped inaugurate that pseudo-proprietory

Circulars like this, picturing Saengerfest Hall that stood on the present Music Hall site, advertised the Cincinnati Industrial Exposition of 1874. The broadsides listed 36 hotels — all now gone — offering accommodations at a top of $4 a day.

UNDER THE DIRECTION OF A BOARD OF COMMISSIONERS APPOINTED BY THE

Board of Trade, Chamber of Commerce and Ohio Mechanics' Institute.

This Exposition is Supported by a Public Guarantee Fund, OF A QUARTER OF A MILLION, and is in no sense a Private Enterprise.

tradition, and gentry advocates in the 1840s and 1850s of "public" services such as fire departments, the police, and parks, followed that model as closely as possible, though in most cases, and much to their chagrin, they lost control by the 1870s to city and state authorities because of the dominant role of taxes in financing those operations. By the last quarter of the 19th century, then, members of the gentry elite might approach the municipality for resources, but they thought in pseudo-proprietory terms, preferring to keep the institutions under their own rather than democratic control. It was such thinking which formulated the solution to the problem of creating suitable permanent buildings and a location for the exposition conceived as a great civilizing agent.

The impetus came from Reuben R. Springer, a native from Frankfort, Kentucky, who came to Cincinnati early in the 19th century and amassed a fortune in the retail, wholesale, and general merchandise business of his father-in-law, Henry Kilgour, and by shrewd investments in local real estate, railroad stocks, banks, and insurance companies. A devout Catholic whose contributions helped finance St. Peter in Chains Cathedral, Springer's beneficent interests also included the arts. He was a close friend of George Ward Nichols and John Shillito, a wealthy Cincinnati department store merchant and a Music Festival Trustee, to whom he wrote in May of 1875 a letter outlining a plan for placing the exposition musical festival on an enduring foundation.

Heading his letter "Some views about a Music Hall Building," Springer contended that such an edifice should be built on the current exposition site, and that because "there is something in a name" it should be called Music Hall, a reference either to the success of the Musical Festival which he proposed housing in the hall, or to the exposition committee's use of that name for one of its buildings and departments. Springer stipulated as an "indispendable requisite to start it, the city government must give the use of the Elm Street lot at a nominal rent to an incorporated society that must be created to manage and carry out the project." The society should be open to any citizen who paid an initiation fee and an annual contribution, and Springer proposed to place the administration under a board of fifteen or twenty individuals drawn from the membership of the society and appointed by City Council, all serving without pay. He thought "the Musical Hall building" should be simply and inexpensively designed so the society could charge modest rentals yet start its management of the enterprise free of debt. He also wanted it "planned and constructed so as to be capable of being used for exposition purposes in connection with suitable buildings that may be constructed to the north and south . . . ." To help raise the money for the music hall, Springer offered to put up $125,000, but posed two conditions — that the city commit the lot tax free in perpetuity and that an additional $125,000 "is secured by donation from our citizens . . . ." Altogether, Springer's scheme sought to enlist the aid of the municipality and citizens in constructing a civic complex, at least one building, for which he personally contributed $125,000, would be called Music Hall, designed to accommodate exposition exhibits in the fall and the Musical Festival in the spring, and managed and maintained by an incorporated society.

Reuben R. Springer

Some views about a Musical Hall building —

There something in a name; I would call it
"The Cincinnati, Musical Hall Society" —
As an indispensible requisite to start it,
the City Government must give the use
of the Elm Street lot at a nominal
rent to an Incorporated Society that
must be created to manage and carry
out and perpetuate the objects in view —
The lot and improvements must be free
of taxation, at least of Municiple & School
taxes. and State and County, if possible —
there is great propriety in this, as the
ground and improvements will be Owned
by the City, and will be used solely
in the intrests of the people, and for
the public good. —

The charges for the use of the Hall
&c for all proper purposes and public
occasions and meetings, should be as low
as possible, or barely enough to keep

25

the buildings in first rate condition, and
defray the necessary expences of the
Society, on an economical organization —
The Society should be formed of
Citizens <u>unlimited</u> in number, and
who should pay an initiation fee and
an annual sum for the privilege of
Membership, and to which some advantages
should attach of tickets and reserved
seats, for special occasions — This would
form a fund for improvements, and
would also be a Guarantee Fund
for any deficiencies that might occur
in giving Musical Festivals &c —

The Administration to be under a &
of Controul of fifteen or twenty members, and
an Executive Committee of five or more as
may be found best — These to be elected
by the Members of the Society, <u>voting in person</u> —
The City Council to have the privilege of naming
            members of Board &c — being the Owners
of the property, this should be conceded

as a matter of right — No Salary
or pay of any kind to be given to
members of either Board — The
power of the Board of Controul and
Executive Board to be defined strictly
in the Bye Laws, —

The Musical Hall Building to be
located in the Centre of the lot, and so
Placed and constructed as to be capable
of being used for Exposition purposes,
in connection with suitable buildings
that may be constructed on the North &
South to the limits of the lot — this
may be a matter for the future, and
will, I think, follow of Course —

The Society should not commence
the enterprise with less than $ 250.000 =
this much secured, would assure Success —

The plans should be strictly made, so that
the estimates of cost should be within the
above sum, so that the Society should start
clear of debt, Bonded or floating —

27

The building should be plain, but very substantial, and care should be observed not to lavish money on mere ornamentation — The attempt to make it fire proof, should not be even entertained; any advantage gained, would be more than counterbalanced by enormous additional expense — Floors laid on mortar, — tile flues — avoiding wooden partitions — iron columns (where needed) in place of wood and tin roof, will make it safe from fire, at least with moderate insurance —

I think it of great importance that the society should be clear of debt when the buildings are finished; otherwise it might be necessary to impose heavy charges for the use of the Hall, and thereby to a great extent impair its usefulness, put in jeopardy the whole enterprise — there is no profit or satisfaction for any thing

if loaded with debt — this should be
kept — carefully in view. — These
remarks are merely suggestive, and
intended to elicit information and
bring out the experience of those
more capable of giving what may
be valuable in making the enterprise
a success. —

Now to the main point; I
will donate in money, (payable as
the work progresses) one half of
the before named sum, say One
hundred and twenty five thousand
dollars. ($125.000.) on two conditions;
First, that the lot is secured in
perpetuity for the uses of the Society,
at a nominal rent, and free of
taxation as before named; and
Secondly that a sum of not less
than One hundred and twenty five
thousand dollars ($125.000.) is
secured by donations from our

Citizens; failing either of these
my offer is withdrawn. — All
other matters except these two I
leave to the wisdom of those who
may be chosen to manage the enterprise —
I will add that I do not wish
to take any part in carrying out the
enterprise, either in the Board or Committee
or other Office, active or honorary —
My advanced age and the many calls
I now have on my time, will I think
be a sufficient reason, for thus de-
-clining, in advance any share in
the labour — I also desire that
may name shall only be known
as a donor, among, I hope, hund.
of others — I have taken the liberty
of addressing this communication to you, as
one who has been most active & efficient
in musical enterprise, and to take such
action about it, as you may deem best —

To
John Shillito Esq.

R. R. Springer

Springer's proposition enthralled the originators of the musical festival. Shillito took the plan to the Music Festival Association board, which in turn communicated with the Chamber of Commerce, Board of Trade, and OMI, the sponsors and managers of the annual expositions. Representatives from each of these three groups sat down informally with Springer to iron out a subscription form satisfactory to all those interested in the grand exposition and music festival idea. It stated that those agreeing to contribute sought to raise money to build a Music Hall "for encouraging and cultivating a taste for music and holding musical festivals, and capable also of being used for expositions, exhibitions of art, fairs and public meetings or entertainments of any kind not prohibited by law," a formulation of the proposition which ignored the issue of additional new buildings and by implication jeopardized the grand scale of the expositions. Nonetheless, the subcription forms appeared in the daily press on May 26, and no one objected when representatives of the four groups met three days later in formal session to discuss methods of raising the money.

The unanimity, however, soon collapsed. The next meeting, on June 1st, heard objections to the form of the subscription solicitation as "subordinating the interests and importance of the Expositions to those of the music festival." After some negotiations the group changed the form so that it asked donations "for the purpose of building a Music Hall for encouraging and cultivating a taste for music, and holding Musical Festivals, Expositions of Industry, and Art, also for holding such fairs and public meetings or entertainments of any kind not prohibited by law." This statement, too, failed to satisfy the exposition advocates, who first began to encourage their supporters to give money for the construction of wings to the building suitable for housing machinery, horticultural, and artistic exhibits, and then started to circulate a separate subscription list, thus endangering the prospects for raising the $125,000 matching Springer's offer. To counter this move, Springer, on June 7th, wrote a public letter in search of a more cohesive compromise.

He began by pointing to the confusion about his objective, which he felt had reached such proportions as to make the failure of the undertaking not only possible but probable, conceding that perhaps the "name may have something to do with it." He asserted that he always intended the building for exposition uses and that on its completion the grand exposition accommodations would be "one-half, if not two-thirds secured." He had also intended, at the proper time, to assist in the completion of the industrial buildings, defining the proper time as the moment when the matching $125,000 for music hall had materialized. To allay the fears of grand exposition supporters he pledged publicly that after securing from contributors the matching $125,000 for music hall, he would guarantee $50,000, paying it as the work progressed, "to be expended in the erection of suitable and permanent buildings around the hall for the purpose of holding Industrial Expositions, or for other uses connected with the public welfare." To the pledge, however, he attached a string. His $50,000 for additional exposition space would be forthcoming only if "our citizens" contributed another $100,000.

The letter weakened without entirely dissipating the objections of what had become known as "the Exposition party." Springer resisted subsequent attempts to unite the subscriptions, but agreed to sign another subscription form soliciting funds for "buildings additional to a Music Hall, which additional buildings and said Music Hall are to be erected and used for encouraging a taste for music and holding music festivals, concerts, expositions of industry and art, also for holding such fairs and public meetings, or entertainments of any kind not prohibited by law." A string dangled from this form as well, for it would not bind contributors until after Springer's original proposition for financing Music Hall has been fulfilled.

That maneuver ended attempts to raise money separately for the wings to the building, but it did not produce a surge of contributions for either Music Hall or its wings. Until November of 1875, the music festival adherents remained in doubt, almost despair, about their prospects for success. To overcome the tardiness in securing matching subscriptions, which then stood at $90,000, Springer agreed to add $20,000, the amount needed to bring the citizen's matching fund for Music Hall proper to $125,000, guaranteeing $250,000 for the project and therefore activating Springer's other pledge of $50,000 to head the drive for $150,000 toward the addition of wings to complete the grand exposition project.

Within a month of publication of this letter the citizens' matching fund for music hall mounted to the magic figure of $125,000. But one other difficulty forced another alteration of Springer's original scheme. His proposition of May, 1875, required the city to commit the lot south of the exposition grounds, as well as the exposition grounds themselves, as a site for the complex. The city, however, did not own the extra lot, then valued at $50,000, and the state of municipal finances made its purchase an "unreasonable request" which, if insisted upon, might "defeat the enterprise" by discouraging the city's willingness to turn over, without charge, the exposition grounds to the management of another corporation. Supporters of the project, including Springer, therefore set aside that part of the proposal, reasoning that additional ground would not be needed until "our citizens" stood ready to add "supplemental buildings for exposition purposes." They also decided, since the money for the new hall came from "citizens of Cincinnati" and the land from the municipal corporation, that the building should be known as "the Cincinnati Music Hall," thereby virtually eliminating the possibility of naming it after Springer or of its being referred to as simply the music hall of the Cincinnati Industrial Exposition.

While efforts to raise money for the wings continued, Springer on the first day of December, 1875, called together the contributors to Music Hall to decide upon a plan for the organization of the managing society. The assemblage appointed a committee to handle the task, which reported on December 8, recommending the incorporation of fifty of the contributors, selected by the orginial subscribers from those among their number willing to take stock at once, or from among subscribers willing to take stock after the initial offer, each stock holder to have one vote for each dollar contributed to the subscription. The corporation would be called the Cincinnati Music Hall Association, would be non-profit, and closed in that no stock could be sold or bequeathed outside the first group of stockholders without first offering the stock to the members of the corporation, and then only after securing approval by the seven trustees of the person to whom the stock would be transferred. The corporation should be formed for the purpose of "erecting, maintaining, and establishing a public hall . . . for musical festivals, concerts, expositions of art or industry, fairs, conventions or public meetings, and such other entertainments as may not be prohibited by law" or deemed improper by the trustees. To this end all money raised at the time of incorporation or collected in the future to build additions to the hall would be placed in charge of the trustees. The contributors approved the committee's work without reference in any way to the additional buildings or wings necessary for the realization of the grand exposition conception, leaving only negotiations with the city over securing access to the exposition grounds as an obstacle to the consummation of the deal.

Talks with the city proved more protracted and tedious than the backers of the project anticipated. Part of the problem rested with the Association's demand for broad powers for managing the grounds and use of the building, and with the growing tendency, exhibited as recently as 1873 during discussions between City Council and another society for the use of city property as a zoological gardens, for municipal officials to control more closely the activities of individuals banded together in various corporations, ranging from street railways to gas companies, which offered services to residents. The other difficulty stemmed from the failure of the incorporation plan to mention any buildings or wings except the main hall, an oversight which once more jeopardized the grand exposition idea.

Finally, on April 3, 1876, the two parties reached a settlement of their differences. Although the agreement did not, as Springer originally hoped, provide for city representation of the association's governing body, it altered significantly the plan as envisaged by the incorporators. By its terms the Association paid $1.00 to secure continuing access to, but not legal ownership of, the exposition site, free of taxes, charges, or assessments of any kind. But the Association had to agree that the buildings would be subject to visitation by the police, to the execution of ordinances relating to the peace and good order of the city, and that it would not interfere with the duty of the Park Board or other body or authority having charge of the parks, to protect and keep the grounds in good order. And section three of the agreement stipulated that as soon as either the additional $150,000 or a "sufficient" amount had been raised the Association would erect further buildings "as may be fit, necessary and proper for the larger and more complete accommodation of expositions of industry and art," and connect them with the "main hall."[5]

Despite the bickering, delays, compromises, and postponements attending the creation of the edifice, the grand opening of the Cincinnati Music Hall at the Musical Festival of 1878 dazzled contemporaries. Nichols called it "transcendently successful," noting however the difficulty of measuring "the scope of its influence, covering, as it does, a wide area, embracing the interests of commerce and civilization as well as those of morals and the art of music." Nonetheless, Murat Halstead, the editor of the *Cincinnati Commercial,* gave it a try. To him the event demonstrated that "Cincinnati is the central city of the Nation."

As director of music in Cincinnati schools, Charles Aiken developed the children's choruses that participated in early May Festivals and led a campaign through which Cincinnati school children contributed some $3,000.00 to the building of Music Hall.

This statue of Theodore Thomas, first music director of the May Festival, stands in the foyer of Music Hall. President William Howard Taft made the dedicatory address at the 1910 festival. Thomas conducted the festivals from 1873 to 1904.

33

It is one of the cosmopolitan places . . . the center of a constellation of cities . . . Cincinnati has for some years been growing in favor with the people who surround her, as has appeared in the great delegations that have visited us on festival and business excursions . . . The Music Hall will increase our attractiveness . . . and joined to the incomparable advantage of our location, and the known development of our hotel accomodations, it will command a vast variety of conventions — political, religious, benevolent and scientific . . . [and] for the first time we shall realize the full value of our geographical situation. Washington will remain our political and New York our commercial capital, but Cincinnati will be the City of National Conventions and the social center and musical metropolis of America.

For almost a decade Halstead's view of the roles of Music Hall as the centerpiece in a grand exposition complex seemed credible. In 1878, Nichols incorporated a college of music, giving the city three music schools, enticed

Theodore Thomas to serve as its musical director, and located the institution on the third floor of the Music Hall. In 1879, the North American Saengerbund selected the hall as the site of its Saengerfest. By that year, too, and just in time for the Cincinnati Industrial Exposition of 1879, the first since 1875 and an event which took place annually until 1888, both the south and north wings of the building had been completed, filling the lot between Twelfth and Fourteenth Streets and fulfilling the original conception of the exposition organizers. In the summer of 1880 the Democratic Party held its presidential nominating convention in the main hall, and the building accommodated other assemblages in this period as well, including the biennial Musical Festivals, the crowds which turned out to hear religious evangelists Sam Small and Sam Jones, and the civic protest meeting which inadvertently served as staging a ground for a lynch mob quelled by militia in the Court House "riot" of 1884 during which fifty of the participants died and over 200 suffered injuries.

Yet by the end of the decade an era in the history, the exposition site, Music Hall, and of the city had passed.

Serving its original role as an exposition center as well as a concert hall — wings flanking the central building were specifically designed for the purpose — Music Hall saw one of its' most successful industrial expositions in 1879, with over a thousand exhibitors. President Rutherford B. Hayes gave the dedicatory address, just as he had at the first exposition nine years earlier when he was governor of Ohio.

The industrial exposition of 1888, touted as the Centennial Exposition of the Ohio Valley and Central States and held in commemoration of the settlement of Cincinnati, proved both the most spectacular and the last of the series. Three cities, fifteen states, the federal government, and five foreign countries participated, and for the occasion the commissioners added to the exposition complex a cruciform Main Exposition building in Washington Park connected to Music Hall by bridges over Elm Street, a Machinery Hall over the canal behind Music Hall, and an Agricultural Hall. But the centennial exposition closed on a sober note, leaving a debt incurred by its failure to attract masses of visitors and a chastened president, who commented distastefully in his report that . . .

> *An exhibition of Arts and Industries, pure and simple, no matter of what excellence, fails, in large measure, to attract or satisfy the general public. . . . It was not until I was prevailed upon . . . to introduce . . . certain forms of light amusements, that any appreciable increase in attendance was noted . . . .*

As the introduction of "light amusements" to the "exhibits" in the celebration of 1888 suggests, the age of expositions conceived of as exhibits expressing and encouraging the progress and unity of the "arts and morality" among the productive though not entirely civilized classes of society in and around one of four or five centers of civilization in America had terminated, and the age of great urban and international fairs, construed as entertaining diversions illustrating the accomplishments of specialists in discreet areas of essentially professional expertise, and as demonstrations of the "maturity" of a national culture had arrived. Such fetes Cincinnatians proved unwilling or unable to conduct. The chief obstacle, however, lay not in the city's alleged "conservatism," but with Cincinnati's place in the new system of cities and with a new perception of the nature and functioning of society.

By the 1880s heavy industry dominated the nation's economy, and the geographical and organizing core — the heart or central unit — of the new industrial society stretched in a corridor from New York through Pittsburgh and across the cities of the Great Lakes through Chicago

THE COLLECTION OF PAINTINGS IN THE ART GALLERY.

OHIO.—THE SEVENTH INDUSTRIAL EXPOSITION OF CINCINNATI IN THE GRAND PERMANENT BUILDINGS, SEPTEMBER 1876 TO OCTOBER 1876.

in the west. Here stood the places of most rapid and diverse growth between 1880 and 1920, the great cities with both the highest per capita incomes and the most rapidly burgeoning and cosmopolitan populations. They attract not only the bulk of the southern and eastern European immigrants but also adapted technological innovations most rapidly and became the artistic centers and leading repositories of high culture in the country. Not surprisingly, Chicago housed the World's Columbian Exposition of 1893, one of the first of the great new fairs conducted in America.

At the same time a new view of society took hold. It saw nations as collections of social organisms consisting of specialized and differentiated parts arranged in a hierarchy which, through coordination at the top, worked together for the welfare of the whole. Each of the constituent units, moreover, marched to its own rhythm and pursued its own logic, so that organized capital, management and labor, each of the professions, each of the arts, each of the races, and each of the classes possessed its own function, place, and its own separate but equal identity. The same kind of thinking defined the territorial organizing units of society, a mode of thought which stacked in logical progression neighborhood, city, section and nation.

In this new metropolitan and intellectual milieu the problem of Cincinnati's and the exposition site's place in the larger system of which they formed a part looked strikingly different than in the mid- and later decades of the 19th century. In response, Cincinnati civic leaders trimmed their sails and turned inward. Instead of

contending with St. Louis, Chicago, New Orleans and New York for the role of the American metropolis, they now sought to calculate the city's ''natural'' potential for growth and to nurture its internal elements so as to live up to that potential.

Beginning roughly during the last two decades of the 19th century, Cincinnati boosters, while retaining their characteristically florid language, limited their aspirations to making the Queen City queen merely of the Ohio Valley and therefore to earn for it a respectable place as a major city in the new national system and hierarchy of cities. This meant, among other things, putting its government and internal environment in order, an effort which began in the 1880s and climaxed in the 1920s with the adoption of a new city charter, the victory of the Charter Committee in city politics, and the creation of the city's first comprehensive plan. It also meant transforming art and music into ''classics,'' the products and performances of highly trained, skilled and creative individuals, whose work could be understood and appreciated only by persons inducted by study and regular exposure into the mysteries of the specialized forms which the various arts now took. And it also meant transforming the exposition site and its centerpiece, Music Hall, into a place and buildings congruent with the new order of things.

Music Hall has played a part in more than promotion of the arts. A protest meeting there in 1884, voicing public indignation at the sentences meted out in a murder case, led to rioting in which some 50 persons were reported killed and over 200 injured, and to the burning of the courthouse.

MOB IN FRONT OF MUSIC HALL

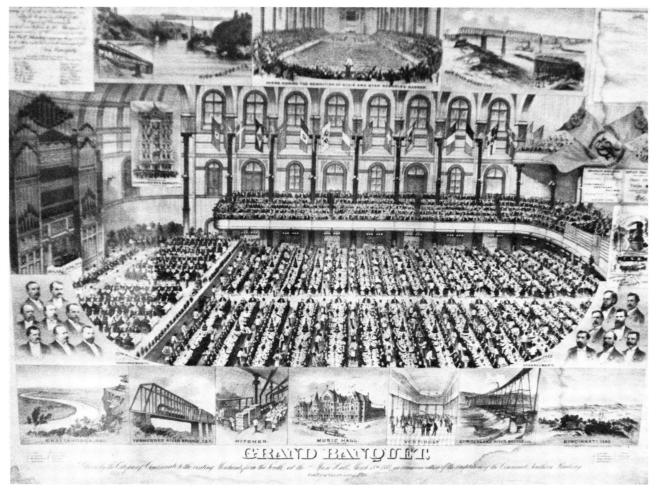

A depiction of the grand banquet celebrating the construction of the Cincinnati Southern Railroad. The event took place on the floor of Music Hall while the guests observed the feast from the balconies.

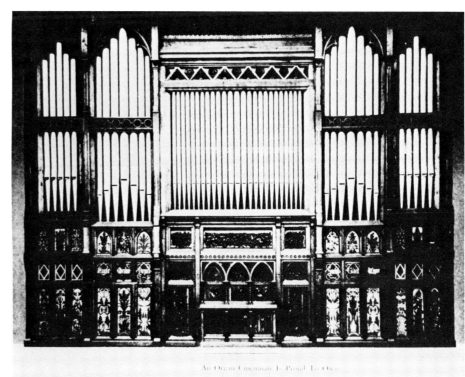

Music Hall changed over the years, and so did its great organ. The concert advertisement pictures it as it was in 1880, (left) the engraving (above) as it was in the 1920s. Some of the original wild cherry woodwork remains.

Music Hall, and temporary buildings in Washington Park and spanning the canal along what is now Central Parkway, sparkled with electric lights for the Centennial Exposition of 1888. The most dramatic feature was the transformation of 1300 feet of the canal into a Venetian waterway so that gondoliers could pole their craft the full length of "Machinery Hall." But the expositions increasingly ran into financial difficulties despite incorporation of "light amusements," and were finally abandoned.

Although the organic mode of thought underlay the idea of locating each of the arts in its own building and neighborhood, achieving that goal in the American urban setting became not merely conceivable but reasonable because of fundamental changes wrought during the late 19th and early 20th centuries in the geographic structure of cities.

The elaboration of horse-drawn street railway systems and the coming of the electric trolley, auto, truck and bus, the steel frame skyscraper, and the electric elevator, accounted for most of these changes. These new technologies fostered a distension in the geographic limits of urban settlements, a reduction in metropolitan building densities, an intensification of land use specialization and the appearance of clearly delimited functional districts, and an unprecedented spatial sorting of people by race, class and ethnicity. In this context the conception of the city as an organic social unit composed of specialized and differentiated parts seemed

compelling, even self-evident. And the persistent outward thrust of residents, industry and commerce continually opened new territory for urban development on the rim of the metropolis and relieved the compression of building near its center, producing a luxurious sense of space and making it possible to think of buildings and sites in single rather than multi-purpose terms.

While Cincinnati's growth rate slackened in the late 19th century, it still ranked in 1900 as the nation's tenth largest city and, like other major metropolises, its spatial structure bore the unmistakeable imprint of the application of the new transport and building technologies. As early as the 1870s, Sidney Maxwell in *Cincinnati and Its Suburbs* apotheosized the glories of life on the cool green rim of the city in Clifton, Avondale and Walnut Hills. By the 1880s and 1890s, moreover, the focus of the central business district had moved up from Third Street and away from its riverfront orientation,

centering now on Fountain Square and anchored unambiguously by a line of ten and twelve story buildings along an east-west axis between the railway terminals and hotels on its flanks. Slums, factories, and warehouses shared the riverfront bottoms and pressed in like pincers on the Over-the-Rhine district from their other bases in the near east and west ends, while the construction of factories on outlying open land spread an arc of industrial communities from Mohawk-Brighton around the city's northern ridge of hills from St. Bernard easterly through Norwood and into Oakley. An aggressive annexation policy pursued by Cincinnati municipal officials brought some of these places within the city's corporate limits, stretching its territory from twenty-two to thirty-five and fifty square miles in 1880, 1890 and 1910 respectively.

In response to this new intellectual and urban environment managers of the exposition site made decisions which altered fundamentally its place and function in the city's life.

In 1895, facing three successive deficits, the board decided to abandon irrevocably the grand exposition idea by remodeling, to the neglect of the wings, the main hall to make it more suitable for musical events, but without destroying its utility as a "convention hall, or a place to hold large political, religious and other meetings." That decision ended Music Hall's history as a combined music, convention, and exposition center, relegating the last function exclusively to the wings of the edifice. It also tied the main building's fate to its ability to become a "proper Music Hall," placed it in competition with other similar facilities in the city, and coincided with the appearance in the Association's annual reports from the later 1890s of the terms "Springer Hall," or "Springer Music Hall," to distinguish the renovated building's past association with the grand exposition idea.

The appelation "Springer Hall" did not stick, but the trustees managed to raise enough money to transform the exposition's main hall into a place closely resembling in form and function New York's Carnegie Hall. According to their estimates the remodeling would cost $100,000, a sum they found almost as difficult to raise as did their predecessors in collecting the matching grant for Springer's original contribution in 1875. But they found a way. After completion of the new exposition site in 1878, Springer gave the Association railway stocks, the earnings of which he wished used to meet deficits and to defray maintenance cost in the interest of keeping rentals for the exposition facilities as low as possible. To meet the $100,000 remodeling cost the board agreed in 1895 to appropriate at least $60,000 of the money earned from Springer's stock and its income on the condition that subscribers put up the other $40,000, all of which principal would be repaid at four percent interest per annum with earnings accumulated from the Springer stock and from selling off the board's other investments. This practice not only differed from the 1875 subscription in that those earlier "matching" contributors made outright gifts to the Association. It also required the board to raise the money outside the Association membership, for as shareholders in the non-profit corporation they could not legally profit by its activities.

The board managed to raise the $40,000 subscription, but it soon faced another problem. The original cost estimates for remodeling fell short by $20,000, an overrun occasioned by the decision to add stage fittings necessary for opera, a musical form which came into vogue among the cultivated classes in the United States during the late

A PRIVATE GARAGE SPOILING A HOME STREET.
Doors swing over street and garage masks houses.

The Cincinnati city plan of 1925 touted the virtues of the new legal device of zoning as a means of controlling the urban development. (Left and Top)

SIMILAR PRIVATE GARAGE AS CONTROLLED BY ZONING

19th century. As it turned out, the board possessed some reserves beyond its pledge of $60,000, and met the rest by securing a subscription loan from an individual and a $4,000 gift from the Cincinnati Musical Festival Association, sponsors of the biennial event under the baton of Theodore Thomas which by the 1890s was known as the May Festival. The Festival Association expected to recoup its gifts from the next two festivals, giving Music Hall at the least a biennial tenant for the next four years. And by 1895 the prospects of picking up an annual customer looked bright, for in the mid-1890s women from the city's fashionable outlying districts were spearheading a drive to establish in Cincinnati a permanent symphony orchestra of the "classical" variety, one with top-flight musicians and leadership recruited nationally and internationally as well as locally, the standard source of talent for former Cincinnati orchestras.

Impetus for the classical symphony campaign came from the Ladies Musical Club, a group formed in 1891 for the musical education, rather than the edification, of its members and other interested individuals. By 1894 the Club's associate members numbered 300, and that year the Club decided to take the lead in securing for

Cincinnati a permanent symphony orchestra. To that end the women set up a male advisory committee to raise and manage the funds, established the Cincinnati Orchestra Association with Mrs. William Howard Taft in the chair, secured the support of Charles P. Taft, editor of the *Times-Star,* and opened negotiations designed to unite the factions in the city's musical establishment, including especially the College of Music and the Musical Festival Association, which had been at loggerheads since the 1880s when Theodore Thomas left the College but retained his connection with the May Festival. In 1895 the first series of concerts by a Cincinnati classical symphonic orchestra, a unit its founders hoped would "compete favorably with any in the country," took place in Pike's Opera House.

From the beginning of the effort to remodel Music Hall, its board hoped that "radical changes" in the building would make it a model of its kind, one which would not only help the hall "regain its former prestige" but also "become the home of the Orchestra Association, the Appollo and Orpheus clubs, and kindred musical organizations in this city . . ." The Orchestra

Association, for its part, wanted to enlarge significantly the class of persons which appreciated classical symphonic music, as well as to establish a permanent symphony on a solid foundation. For those purposes it desired a concert hall with a large seating capacity, and Music Hall, with its 3462 places, seemed ideal. The two boards therefore agreed to present the 1896-97 symphony concerts in Music Hall, reasoning that since "the orchestra is a public institution, which belongs to the city, it should properly find its home in Music Hall, which was built for the people of Cincinnati, and dedicated to their use." The Orchestra Association acknowledged, however, that Music Halls' dimensions dwarfed both the fifty-four piece orchestra and its limited audiences, but argued that "our work is an educational one, and its object is partly defeated when there is no opportunity of opening a large part of the house to the public at much lower prices than . . . possible" during the previous season.

For several groups and reasons, then, the remodeling of Music Hall proved propitious. It made it possible for the Ladies Musical Club through the Orchestra Association to expand its educational mission by enlarging the number

Decreasing reliance on the river as a means of transportation led to a shift of the heart of downtown Cincinnati from the riverfront to the area of Fountain Square, pictured here in the early 1900s.

of potential recruits for initiation into the musical aspect of turn-of-the-century high culture. It forwarded the internal urban reform campaign by providing a mechanism for improving the sophistication and expertise and increasing the size and broadening the socio-economic scope of the cultivated class. It contributed to the booster effort to render the city eligible for membership in the ranks of the nation's major metropolitan centers by giving it both a first-class music hall and creating a showcase for the city's permanent classical symphony, an institution deemed indispensable for distinguishing first-rate cities from lesser places. And it also gave the Music Hall Association, for the time being at least, a regular tenant.

The regular fare of May Festivals, Cincinnati Symphony Orchestra concerts, and local and regional business expositions held in the building's annexes dominated the use of Music Hall buildings into the 1920s, although Music Hall lost its role as home of the symphony orchestra. The symphony stopped performing in 1907 as the consequence of a dispute between the Orchestra Association and the musicians' union over both wage scales and the importation of outside players. The Association decided to disband the orchestra rather than reach a compromise settlement with the union. Within a year, however, the Association undertook to revive the orchestra, hoping to secure as a home a smaller hall more suitably proportioned for its usual audiences of 800 to 2000 persons. That same year Mary M. Emery, the widow of an industrial and real estate millionaire, donated $500,000 to the Ohio Mechanics Institute for the construction on Walnut between Canal and Twelfth Street, a site just six blocks from Music Hall, of a new building, the plans for which included an assembly facility to be known as "Emery Auditorium." She offered the space as a home for the revived symphony, which resumed its concerts in Music Hall in 1909 and moved to the just-completed Emery Auditorium in 1912, utilizing Music Hall through the 1920s only for occasional special concerts.[6]

The Music Hall Association survived the loss, drawing solace from the selection of its facilities as the location for the "World in Cincinnati" Christian missionary exposition of 1912. This kind of spectacle took place in several American cities during the early 20th century, and apart from their religious purposes, also served, as Professor Henry D. Shapiro has observed, as a means by which contemporaries studied and sorted out people from other regions and civilizations. As part of the show in Cincinnati the event's organizers divided the South Annex into departments, each of them dedicated to one geo-racial area of missionary endeavor. Within the partitioned sections visitors could view exhibits of the diverse ways of life missionaries encountered in Hawaii and Puerto Rico, two of the United States' more recent non-continental territorial acquisitions, on the prairie and mining frontiers, in rural districts and big cities, and among southern Blacks, mountaineers, immigrants, American Indians, and Eskimos. Though seemingly an exotic affair, the concept behind this aspect of the "World in Cincinnati" exposition was in fact "normal," for it brought the "regional" culture of other places to Cincinnati, a location itself now conceived by its inhabitants as the dominant social unit of its own "region," an area which demonstrated its coherence and civilization during the early 20th century through the Fall

Music Hall didn't acquire a stage and proscenium arch until a renovation in 1895-96.

Festivals and other local expositions inaugurated after 1900 on the old grand exposition site, and through the May Festival and symphony concerts which graced Music Hall after the remodeling of the 1890s.

By accommodating these various events in its buildings the Music Hall Association remained solvent and preserved its property from dilapidation through the first quarter of the 20th century. It received some assistance, moreover, from forces outside its ranks, particularly in protecting its location as an institution in but not of the Over-the-Rhine neighborhood. That section of Cincinnati in the early 20th century drifted slowly toward the status of an inner-city slum. Its gradual abandonment as a popular place of residence for musicians affiliated with the symphony provided one index of the change. Others included the expansion north and west of the central business district, the demise as a silk-stocking residential district of the West End from Garfield Place to Dayton Street, the appearance in and around those places of small contingents of southern and eastern European immigrants and poor while rural migrants, and the northerly advance of the lower West End black ghetto. By the 1920s, in short, Over-the-Rhine bore many of the hallmarks of blight, including an aging housing stock, and a mixture of land uses as well as a tightening noose of poor, black, and immigrant individuals, characteristics which planners and sociologists of that era regarded as the prelude to a neighborhood's inevitable descent from stability and respectability into the disorder and tawdriness of a slum.

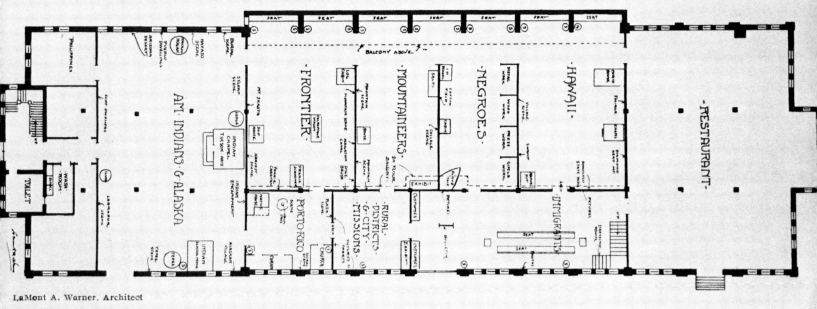

LaMont A. Warner, Architect

Hall of the Home Land, "The World in Cincinnati."
First Floor, South Hall, Music Hall Buildings

*A floor plan of the South Annex during the "World in
Cincinnati" Christian Missionary Exhibit of 1912 indicated
the targets of missionary efforts.*

But the elaboration by city government between 1900 and 1930 of a system of outer- and inner-city parks connected by a network of automobile pleasure drives designed as parks and called parkways preserved the splendid isolation of the music hall buildings from their surrounding residential, commercial, and industrial environment. Specifically, this process covered the canal, transformed its intra-city bed into a circular route for an electric inter-urban connector and its surface into the Central Parkway link between Washington Park and parks on the urban periphery to the north, east and west. It also ultimately thrust Lincoln Park Drive directly west from Music Hall to a projected Union Terminal for railroads, a development which upon its completion gave travelers as they disembarked from their trains a panoramic view of the city centering on Music Hall, while providing visitors to Music Hall a vista which looked west along a broad, tree lined boulevard to the art deco railway station at its foot. Though the inter-urban "subway" was never completed, the other projects gave the music hall buildings a distinctive ambiance as part of the city's park system, identifying their educational and organized recreational functions with the early 20th century conception of the utility of parks and their service role as city-wide and regional rather than local and parochial. Music Hall in the early 20th century was seen as a metropolitan, in the new sense of that word, rather than as a neighborhood institution, a facility which operated as a centralizing and co-ordinating force in the larger organism of which it formed a part, tying the past to the present and the elements of neighborhood, city, metropolis and region to each other while providing a display case for and symbol of the compatibility of high culture and 20th century urban-industrial civilization in America and the Ohio Valley and tri-state region.

By the mid-1920s, however, the Music Hall Association faced another crisis, this one precipitated ironically by the municipal government which otherwise served it so well. In the 1870s Reuben Springer and his associates could legitimately cut corners in designing the grand exposition buildings by neglecting to install costly architectural embellishments for fire protection and sanitation. But the widespread adoption after that date of indoor plumbing, not merely as a private luxury but as a community necessity in the interest of public health, and the recognition of community responsibility for even minor private architectural detail in the interest of public safety, increasingly brought municipal authority to bear on the interior and structural characteristics of private as well as public and quasi-public edifices. The instrument for public intervention in these matters was the building code, and by the 1920s every respectable major city, including Cincinnati, had one. Though often fitfully enforced, self-styled reform administrations, or "boss" governments under pressure from reformers, sought sporadically to bring the meaning of the law into line with its spirit by vigorous inspection campaigns and the conscientious issuance of enforcement orders. In the mid-1920s the building inspectors came to Music Hall and its annexes. They found them, especially the latter, grossly deficient, catalyzing thereby a fiscal crisis, the consolidation of the complex's 20th century identity, and the organizing of a jubilee celebration of the building's 50th anniversary.

Between 1923 and 1928, while worrying about the "severe competition" Emery Auditorium and a new Masonic Temple Building posed for Music Hall, the

trustees addressed themselves to the challenge, and the outcome helps demonstrate the distance between the last quarter of the 19th and the first quarter of the 20th century. With the support and encouragement of the Chamber of Commerce, the Association in 1926 went on record in favor of raising $600,000 for the "reconstruction" of the Music Hall annexes. The money, however, came neither from subscriptions, as in the 1870s, nor from subscription loans, as in the 1890s, but as a consequence of an ingenious arrangement with the city of Cincinnati, then governed by the reform administration of Mayor Murray Seasongood, the product of a coalition among the good government Charter Committee, regular Democrats, and some elements of organized labor.[7]

The municipal assistance came indirectly, for the city had since 1910 operated in a financial straitjacket imposed by new state limits on municipal indebtedness and by the so-called Smith Act, a state law sharply curtailing the city tax rate and mandating the division of local revenues for the county, the city, and the public schools through a budget commission representative of all three governments. To get around these restrictions the city and the Association renegotiated their agreement of 1876, redefining the commitment of the exposition site to the Association as a sale and stipulating that the Association, in return for spending at least $400,000 for remodeling the buildings, could mortgage the property as security for a loan of not more than $750,000, payable within thirty years, for the exclusive purpose of defraying reconstruction expenses and paying interest on the loan during construction. The new agreement also gave City Council the right at any time after January 1, 1937, to require a reconveyance of the title to the property, subject to the terms of the mortgage, the agreement of 1876, or such other agreement as might be reached by the parties.

Invigorated by this municipal transfusion of community capital, the Association's trustees carried out the third major remodeling of the old grand exposition site. When the wraps came off the new facility the first floor of each annex served as sites for the social and business "shows" of the trade associations which Herbert Hoover apotheosized in the 1920s, while the upper floor of one functioned as a combined boxing, wrestling and basketball arena, a local reflection of the growing national interest in mass spectator sports as a profession and potential vocation as well as a diversion, and the other principally as a grand ballroom which as the Topper Club endeared itself to a generation of popular music lovers who danced as they watched and listened to the musicians and each other through the era of the legitimation of Dixieland jazz and its variants. The May Festival and occasional symphony concerts continued to occupy Music Hall, providing for a different audience professional musical performances of another kind, equally prized for their educational and for their pleasurable value. In a candid and discerning remark, the president of the Association in 1928 called the new and reunified complex a "place of entertainment."

That same year Music Hall hosted the "Greater Cincinnati Industrial Exposition," and the exposition as a whole, in a manner reminiscent of the mode of thought which created the "World in Cincinnati" exposition of 1912, presented a picture of the cultures of the metropolitan region as a natural evolutionary development of organic community from the primitive to the modern stage.

Deterioration matching that of Music Hall itself affected the whole area westward across Central Parkway. The turning point came with the building of Union Terminal and Lincoln Park Drive, then the Laurel Homes public housing project of 1938 along the drive, and finally the Queensgate development.

LAUREL HOMES PR...
CINCINNATI,
NEG. No. 14...
AUG. 8, 1938.

This photo, taken in 1920, shows workmen installing the
inter-urban subway connector in the old canal bed under what
is now Central Parkway. Music Hall, with residential
buildings on either side, stands in the center background.

Although business exhibits abounded, the emphasis at the exposition fell on the representation of Music Hall as an essentially musical facility from the very beginning, and on various factors, agents, and persons which in the city's past had acted as educators in and developers of community. The *Golden Jubilee Souvenir Book* for example, contained biographies of the four men whose statues stand in the buildings' foyer — Springer, the philanthropist, Theodore Thomas, the conductor, Charles Aiken, the first superintendent of music in the Cincinnati Public Schools, and Stephen Collins Foster, an occasional resident of Cincinnati in the 19th century and the creator, as the *Souvenir* put it, "of 'The Old Folks At Home,' 'Old Black Joe,' 'The Old Kentucky Home' and other classics in folksong." The *Souvenir* also included a history of the buildings stressing what it interpreted as the historic widespread popular response to appeals for funds for their construction and remodeling and community support of events accommodated therein, making them appear therefore as democratic rather than elite institutions. The "Special Features" of the exposition, moreover, touted not Cincinnati's industrial or commercial prowess or progress, but concentrated on modern modes of transportation, such as the railroad, telephone and airplane, and the history of the "cultural" progress of the area, from the Mound Builders through the age of the frontiersmen, into the era of the creation of folk tales and music as represented in the Foster Memorial, and on to the age of technology and high speed communications.

Perhaps the most characteristic piece of the exposition was the *Souvenir's* brief account of the "growth of musical Cincinnati." It attributed the city's alleged pre-eminence as a center of high culture to regional environmental factors, especially the rolling terrain, winding rivers, beautiful vistas and, "at least in early times," a climate "bracing and invigorating at all seasons." These influences, the *Souvenir* contended, imbued the population with "a tendency toward the fine arts, and so there gradually evolved that certain personality which every community possesses, but which in Cincinnati became so marked that the world today knows this city as patron of fine arts; a mecca of music, with all its ramifications and institutions which have become identified with the personality of Cincinnati." The author conceded that the quality of musical performances in the very early 19th century might not have been elevated, but noted that music "then, like everything else, was in a primitive stage and it was not until some years later, when Cincinnati had acquired some pretensions as a small city, that it was made worth while for a musician to take up his lot here." The implication was clear. The development of the city as a social organism in a benevolent physical environment brought with it a corresponding development of taste and sophistication, and ultimately a full blooming appreciation of "regional" culture, including an interest and proficiency in not only the fine arts but also the folks arts, a set of assumptions which permitted the statues of Theodore Thomas and Stephen Foster to rest comfortably together in a complex of buildings which housed both the May Festival and the Topper Club.

The Topper Club proved a valuable addition to Music Hall, rental income from it in some years exceeding that derived from all other tenants combined. But it scarcely compensated for the loss in 1929 to the newly constructed

William E. Fay, a Cincinnati artist who had studied under Duveneck, prepared this frontispiece for the souvenir program which marked Music Hall's golden jubilee. The spirits of the composers, clockwise, are Wagner, Schubert, Beethoven, Brahms and Listz.

Taft Auditorium of the Symphony Orchestra's "Pop" concerts, for the drain of philanthropic capital into the $2.5 million endowment for the Cincinnati Institute of Fine Arts, the organization created in the late 1920s to provide in a new way solid and consistent support for the Symphony Orchestra which had relied for years on the beneficence of one or two philanthropic families, or for the dulling impact of the Great Depression on all aspects of life.

The Music Hall Association staggered through the 1930s, struggling for revenue merely sufficient to maintain its property, and at the end of the decade faced financial catastrophe, unable to meet its debts, including payments to its mortgage holders. Once more, this time more directly, the municipal government of Cincinnati, not the city's musical or fine arts establishment, came to the rescue of the Association, and in the process fundamentally altered the nature of the institution.

By the terms of the 1927 deed of the Music Hall property from the city to the Association, title to the site and its buildings plus the mortgage obligations reverted to the city in the event of a default by the Association on its mortgage. This clause left open the way for the negotiation of another agreement by the two parties, an arrangement approved by the District Court of the United States in 1941. The legal legerdemain embodied in the settlement authorized the city to "purchase" for $222,500 the real estate of the Association, while consenting to leave the occupation and management of the property with the Association, subject to the right of the city to terminate that occupancy on 30 days written notice. The Association agreed to use the purchase money to meet court costs, operating expenses for 1941, and to pay off the first mortgage bondholders at the rate of approximately thirty to thirty-one cents for each one dollar face amount of the bonds. The reorganization also made possible the expansion of the Association's board of trustees by authorizing the Mayor of Cincinnati to appoint three, an option not exercised until the early 1970s, and Catholic Archbishop John T. McNicolas, through whom the Association was able to keep after the sale and reorganization Springer's railway stock endowment fund, to appoint one.

Through this scheme the lawyers, courts and the city government kept the Association alive, but barely, for the construction in the 1950s of Cincinnati Gardens, an arena for hockey, ice shows, basketball, circuses, popular music concerts, and exhibits, added to an imposing list of Music Hall competitors which by this time included not only Taft and Emery Auditoriums, but the Albee and Schubert theaters, as well as the Zoo summer operas, inaugurated in the 1920s. Equally distressing, from the Association's perspective, the resumption of urban growth after the depression completed the process of transforming the Music Hall neighborhood into a slum occupied principally by poor white newcomers from the upper South and hemmed in on the west by the expansion of the West End

The Topper Club provided gay times for hundreds of people, and money needed to tide Music Hall over lean years. Pictured is a dance bringing University of Cincinnati students and their dates together at the climax of annual Greek Week celebrations. Automobile shows and "Home Beautiful Expositions" also helped shore up hall finances.

49

black ghetto, which by the end of the 1950s reached all the way from Third Street as far north as Crosley Field, the home of the Cincinnati Reds professional baseball team. Nor did the post-World War II planning activities of the city offer any relief from these grim prospects.

In the midst of the war Cincinnati municipal officials and metropolitan area civic leaders decided to revise the city's 1925 master plan in order not only to accommodate returning veterans but also to place the region in a competitive position with other major urban centers which, like Cincinnati, had suffered severe deterioration as a result of the depression and the diversion of resources into the war effort. By this time, moreover, planners and their allies had given up on the idea of the city as an organism which grew naturally from its inner dynamics. That was the conclusion of those who wrote in 1948 the *Cincinnati Metropolitan Master Plan,* a conclusion based on mid-20th century conventional wisdom holding that "when a city expands beyond a certain size it reaches the point of diminishing returns in terms of the advantages which a city, as a social community, would provide for its inhabitants . . . . When the metropolitan city grows beyond this size there is a progressive multiplication of problems, complexities and inconveniences and of the costs of operation and waste of time, money and human effort."

But the turn of the century planners had not only abandoned the turn-of-the-century conception of the city as an organic community. They had also replaced it with another vision which saw the metropolitan area, in the words of University of Chicago sociologist Morris Janowitz, as a congeries of communities of limited liability into and through which individuals and families moved in rhythm with changing career opportunities and changes in their position in the life cycle. That conception informed the Cincinnati plan of 1948, which proposed the "reorganization" of the metropolitan area to "reintroduce in Cincinnati . . . the advantages of . . . cities of about 20,000 to 40,000 population, self-contained in respect to the everyday life of their inhabitants except for such facilities and services as will continue to be located in or supplied by Cincinnati as the central city, and by institutions serving the Metropolitan Area."[8] And while the plan defined and talked about those interchangeable communities, combining various "neighborhoods" in order to meet the magic 20,000 to 40,000 number, it did so in extraordinarily vague terms. What it concentrated on was reforming the metropolitan transportation system to provide access by residents of the communities to jobs and leisure time pursuits which lay outside their boundaries, on the re-development of the riverfront into a residential-recreational park, on the renewal and compression of the central business district into a tight frame around Fountain Square, on the replacement of the lower West End slums with a commercial and light industrial park later dubbed Queensgate I, and on destroying the middle and upper parts of the West End slum and replacing them with public housing and industrial sites.

The plan of 1948, which was gradually carried out in the 1950s and 1960s, left Music Hall and its neighborhood in a kind of limbo. To be sure, the Hall qualified as an institution serving the metropolitan area, but it lay off the mainstream of the road and expressway network designed to knit together the parts of the area with its core, the central business district, and with its proposed chief connection to the outside world, the airport, then projected for a site in the city's northern suburbs near what was to become I-75. And though Music Hall fell into one of the newly fabricated "communities," a place formed from the merger of the adjacent "neighborhoods" of Washington Park, Liberty Street, and Over-the-Rhine, and called "Uptown" in the planning documents, that community received shorter shrift and vaguer treatment than either the West End or the more outlying communities. Clearly, Music Hall and its neighborhood stood low on the list of post-war urban renewal priorities.

Nonetheless, the Hall experienced a mild revival in the 1950s, thanks largely to the Association's success in wresting fiscal aid from Cincinnati City Council. The Cincinnati Symphony Orchestra, which moved back in during the 1930s, continued to use the facility, and the Association rented part of the facilities to the College of Music's radio and television department and local educational television station, WCET. Still, these tenants and revenue from other activities failed to produce enough income to cover operating costs, let alone to generate funds required for the regular program of maintenance and refurbishing required in a building as old, large and so long neglected. Persistently, as a consequence, the Association turned to the City of Cincinnati for help. In 1953 Council authorized the issue of $150,000 in bonds, and after spending that amount the Association in 1955 prepared a three year program of rehabilitation and improvements costing $690,000. In 1956 Council agreed to put up the money, the Association agreeing in return to place each year for twenty-five years $16,000 of its own money into a "Music Hall Rehabilitation Fund."

In this way the Association managed to improve its properties sufficiently to retain its regular tenants and attract enough exhibits, conventions, and Ballroom clients to keep the Hall functioning into the 1960s, when changed perceptions of the city's needs in a facility of this sort created another crisis. By the mid-1960s, the Hall, as Edgar J. "Buddy" Mack, chairman of the Symphony board put it, had "fallen down into a dump," leading some to call for its demolition and construction of new convention center, which ultimately went up on a downtown plot on the central business district's west flank. Music Hall, however, survived the crisis as a consequence largely of local response to the riot-torn, long, hot summers of the 1960s and a fundamental realignment in the national system of cities in the third quarter of the 20th century.

For a variety of reasons, the locus of most rapid metropolitan growth after World War II shifted from the aging cities of the urban-industrial heartland to newer places around the rim of the continent. The new geography of urbanization had its orgins in the first half of the 20th century, when the nation gradually built up a metropolitan military establishment which preferred bases, training stations and camps on sites around the continent's southern and western rim, and when growing national concern for conservation and the "development" of impoverished and backward regions pumped federal monies into the South, Mountain, and Far West through such programs as TVA. The onset of the Cold War, moreover, with its stress on military preparedness and scientific research in a broad variety of fields, coincided with a shift in the structure of the economy from natural resource and labor intensive heavy industries to "footloose" and research and development oriented light industries staffed by disproportionately large numbers of college education personnel. At the same time "tertiary," or service occupations swelled. Businesses and institutions on the cutting edge of the "post-industrial" economy tended first to gravitate toward metropolitan areas like Boston, which possessed a stock of research universities and centers, then increasingly to places offering climatic, scenic and year round outdoor recreational activities to the well educated white collar classes.

In the 1950s and 1960s, then, cities around the continental periphery, but especially in the South, Southwest, Western Mountain states and California from San Francisco down the coast boomed under the impact of continued defense expenditures, the advent of the space age, the development of the federal interstate highway net, and the burgeoning of commercial airline travel. Air conditioning helped, too, as did the exploitation of cheap energy in the form of hydroelectric power and natural gas and oil. And "quality of life amenities," by which was meant high cultural and other leisure-time activities, followed the flow of people and money to the periphery of the continent and the sunbelt, creating the context for the move of the Dodgers from Brooklyn to Chavez Ravine, the construction of the Astrodome and the establishment of a range of high culture institutions in Houston, the rise of the Dallas Cowboys and the Miami Dolphins, the academic ascent of the University of North Carolina at Chapel Hill, with its Research Triangle, and the renaissance of Aspen as a center for the arts and humanities and a ski resort.

To meet the competition, boosters in older big cities countered not merely with new football, baseball, hockey, and basketball facilities but with determined efforts to revitalize their downtowns. They also strove to build on their high culture advantage by constructing elaborate centers for the performing arts, lush settings for the presentation of symphony concerts, jazz, ballet and modern dance, opera, and theatre. Cincinnati followed suit. In the 1960s its civic leaders moved not only toward the creation of the downtown convention center, a building which would virtually eliminate Music Hall's viability as a place for exhibits and conventions, and a riverfront football and baseball stadium, but also toward the establishment of a coalition to support the making of a center for the performing arts.

Here, as elsewhere, particular features of the metropolitan crises of the 1960s provided the impetus for the appearance of the performing arts coalition. Federally supported urban renewal, expressway and public housing programs initiated during the 1950s uprooted thousands of poor and black citizens from their neighborhoods, creating a rising storm of resentment against the local and national politicians and bureaucrats responsible for formulating and carrying out the programs. The protest took the form of black outrage over Negro removal and reghettoization, and of white backlash against the spread of black residential districts. In response, the Kennedy-Johnson administration adopted a policy of encouraging citizen participation through community councils in urban planning and program development, of concentrating on improving the conditions of life in big city residential neighborhoods. The confluence of these factors in the late 1960s and early 1970s produced

massive civil disorder, and demands for Black Power which evoked from whites mimetic cries of Irish Power, German Power, Italian Power, Polish Power, and Appalachian Power, and which spread the neighborhood organization revolution from black into white communities, white collar and WASPish as well as blue collar and "ethnic," outer-city and inner-suburban as well as outer suburban and exurban. Though the din subsided briefly in the mid-1970s, the institutional and ideological bases for ethnic and neighborhood consciousness remained strong, fed now by the perception of energy, resource, tax revenue and capital shortages which made one group's or neighborhood's gain look inevitably like another's loss.

Cincinnati's experience with the post-war metropolitan crisis broadly resembled that of other places. Here, too, by the mid-1960s, urban renewal had uprooted neighborhoods, pushing blacks out of the bulldozed and partially rebuilt West End, forcing some into the outer edges of the Music Hall neighborhood where they clashed with Appalachians, and more into an old middle class black enclave on Walnut Hills, from where the new ghetto spread through the once solidly white neighborhoods of South Avondale, Evanston, and Corryville to Vine Street, a major artery which in 1970 shielded white Clifton from the black advance. Here, too, the frustration of blacks produced long, hot, tense, and violent summers from 1964 to 1968. Here, too, the uprooting and expansion of the black ghetto and the cry of Black Power generated a revival of white ethnic consciousness dominated by Appalachians and Germans, and a neighborhood organization revolution whose champion advocates included W. Emerson "Dusty" Rhodes of white suburban Delhi Township, Carl Westmoreland of the black inner-city neighborhood of Mt. Auburn, and Robert Brodbeck of the white outer-city community of Westwood. And here, too, some of the city's leadership sought to tame both the neighborhood organization revolution and the black civil rebellion by channeling them into activities designed to benefit both particular communities within the city and the larger metropolitan community, a response which once more saved Music Hall and this time transformed it into a center for the performing arts.

One of the most important and enlightened responses to the metropolitan crisis of the 1960s in Cincinnati was the creation in 1966 of the West End Task Force, composed of representatives from a broad range of organizations and institutions with an interest in securing civic peace. Chaired by Edgar "Buddy" Mack, the Task Force's regular and "augmented" membership included blacks from the West End community, business and religious groups, municipal and school board officials, and delegates from the major downtown churches and businesses. It began its work by concentrating on the cleaning up and beautification of dilapidated 19th century town houses on once elegant Dayton Street and on improving West End traffic conditions which endangered children playing along Lincoln Park Drive and other major thoroughfares. But it soon focused its attention on planning, particularly on the treatment of a piece of West End territory stretching north from City Hall at Eighth and Plum to a point directly across Central Parkway from Music Hall known as Queensgate II.

The planning process and programs for Queensgate II came out of a contract for partnership planning signed by

51

the city, the West End Task Force, and the University of Cincinnati. The University's interdisciplinary research and planning team developed an analysis of Queensgate II as a dying neighborhod occupied by an overwhelmingly black, poor, and aging population. Its plight, the team contended, stemmed essentially from its isolation from its surrounding environment by an expressway, major thoroughfares and public housing, a condition which detracted from its utility for residential and business purposes. The Task Force and the city agreed with this diagnosis, and together the three parties worked out a plan called for development of a balanced community of businesses, non-profit institutions, and educational facilities designed to anchor a socio-economically and racially-mixed residential population, and for the creation of "bridges" to open up easy access to the outside world for the benefit of the new neighborhood's residents. Construction of a Town Center constituted a key element in the plan to make Queensgate II into a "new town-in-town," and it proved attractive enough to garner the support necessary for its early completion, although the means by which it came into being located it across the street from Music Hall instead of at the heart of reconstructed Queensgate II.

The appearance of the Town Center idea coincided with a drive for the transformation of Music Hall into a center for the performing arts which would accommodate the offices and performances of the Orchestra, Zoo Opera, May Festival, and provide dressing rooms, library, conductors' quarters, and solo rooms for those organizations. This remodeling envisaged the entire refurbishment of the building, inside and out, including complete redecoration of the public areas, reconstruction of the stage and pit, and installation of a year-round temperature control system, fire sprinklers, escalators and bars and modern toilet facilities. Most of the start-up money came from two sources: $1,200,000 from the city through the issue of councilmanic bonds and $500,000 from the Corbett Foundation, an agency set up by Mr. and Mrs. Ralph Corbett as a means of distributing for educational and high cultural purposes the fortune acquired by Corbett during the post-World War II suburban boom in his home fixtures business in Cincinnati.

Other contributors, the Corbett Foundation and the city invested substantial additional amounts before the project's completion in 1976, but the initial and critical municipal money came in three installments, and they came in large part because Mack played skillfully on his influential positions with the Orchestra and the Task Force to tie together the reconstruction of Music Hall with that of Queensgate II. His method was to link subtly the drive for high culture with the effort to confront the race question. As Mack later described his municipal lobbying campaign,

> Council did not put a very high priority on this, and we had to fight for it. I argued with Council members privately in Committee sessions, and on the floor of Council. I told them, among other things, that the city spends two a half million dollars of the taxpayer's money on Riverfront Stadium to keep professional baseball and football here, and we can spend a little for other things, too. We did fine for a while, but the last time we approached Council the members wavered. So we arranged a dinner before a concert and I sent handwritten, hand-delivered invitations to all Council members and their spouses. One said he could not come. So I called him and said, "look you S. O. B., you're coming and so's your wife." He came. To top the evening we had Councilman Myron Bush, a black and one of our strongest supporters to this point, to participate in the performance of Aaron Copland's **Lincoln Portrait**. We even gave him a dressing room with a star. He had a beautiful reading voice and performed great. And he was tickled to death. We got the money.

With the rehabilitation of Music Hall underway, Peter Kory, head of the city's Department of Urban Development, began to push for the Town Center. But the project stalled until Corbett offered the city money to construct a parking garage for Town Center and Music Hall on the old hospital lot across from Music Hall if the city would funnel parking profits into the coffers of the Music Hall Association, which still ran annual operating deficits. That arrangement worked out, and its consummation, by making the Town Center feasible, helped solve WCET's space problem, for it had no place in the new Music Hall. Encouraged by the commitment of others to the Music Hall neighborhood, WCET's management secured grants from two older local foundations, the Crosley and Schmidlapp, as the core element of the fund to finance the construction of a television studio and offices on top of the garage as the first component of the Town Center. As the design evolved, architects added a connecting pedestrian bridge between the Town Center and Music Hall, making it possible for Music Hall patrons to park and walk to their entertainment without risking either the dangers of the street in a marginal neighborhood or the hazards of crossing Central Parkway on foot.

By 1976 the garage and WCET phase of Town Center and the entire Music Hall projects were completed, but the Queensgate II plan to improve Music Hall's neighborhood stood virtually on dead center, a victim of the Nixon-Ford administration's decision to call a moratorium on the urban crisis and to dismantle the Kennedy-Johnson administration's urban neighborhood renewal policies. The advent of "stagflation" after the Arab-Israeli war of 1973, moreover, combined with the stultification of Cincinnati's tax base, coerced Council, like city officials elsewhere, to adopt an austerity budget. Although Cincinnati avoided a brush with bankruptcy like that which New York experienced beginning in 1975, Council did so by curtailing allocations for such high visibility municipal services as police and fire protection, health clinics, garbage collection, and street maintenance, as well as for other programs less susceptible to public scrutiny. In spite of growing agitation from the city's black community for action, the realization of the Queensgate II dream seemed a long way off, leaving the superbly refurbished Music Hall surrounded on the west by an almost abandoned slum and on the north and east by a deteriorating Over-the-Rhine district.

The same general set of circumstances placed severe financial constraints on other public and quais-public institutions serving the metropolis. The University of Cincinnati averted fiscal disaster by converting to fully state supported status, becoming in 1977 the last of the great municipal universities to take that way out, but the city's arts establishment, lacking that option, turned to

Council for increased subsidies. Council refused, pleading poverty, and the Mayor and several Council members suggested the arts institutions should call on suburban townships, villages, cities, and the county for aid. That accomplished little, except to embitter an already lively debate among elected officials from all these units of local government over which "community" should support and by how much the broad range of services which the late 20th century metropolis offered its residents.

The Music Hall Association, meanwhile, pursued other avenues of support to cover its annual operating deficits and maintenance programs. It succeeded in 1975 in placing the building on the National Historic Landmark register, a step enabling it to apply through the Ohio Historic Preservation Office for federal funds to cover half the costs of redecorating the interior walls and ceiling of the auditorium in preparation for the celebration in 1978 of the centennial of Music Hall's dedication. The Association also resisted pressure from the Orchestra to reduce its $100,000 rental fee, and fended off charges that the management of the building failed to attract as many other clients as it might. And it engaged in discussions with other arts organizations of how they might together meet the financial crunch, but these talks provided little ground for optimism, despite the existence of a precedent of cooperative action.

The Cincinnati Fine Arts Institute began in the late 1920s as a consortium to support fine arts performances and educational institutions, and for years conducted annual fund raising drives for the benefit of the Orchestra, Taft Museum, Cincinnati Art Museum, and the Opera. That left the Music Hall Association, like the May Festival Association, the Cincinnati Ballet, the Playhouse, and the Contemporary Arts Center, to run their own fund drives, a situation one local arts reporter denounced as "inefficient, duplicative, and . . . divisive . . . ." In the crisis of the mid-1970s the indictment sounded more credible than in the past, and several of the art groups considered consolidating their efforts with the Big Four into one united fine arts fund campaign. But the talks stalled, despite cautious P & G support for the idea, in part because the "independents" feared their solid contributors might not maintain, let alone increase, their past levels of support under such an arrangement.

With the wells of local philanthropy and municipal support apparently dry, the arts organizations looked for an "outside" government subsidy. The state of Ohio seemed unlikely to help, for as one of the states of the declining urban-industrial heartland it faced a fiscal crunch of its own. Beyond that, Ohio historically ranked low — 29th nationally — in its support of the arts. Under these circumstances some local arts' supporters turned hopefully to a proposal of Congressman Frederick Richmond of New York, a former chairman of the managing body of Carnegie Hall. Richmond in 1977 suggested that federal taxpayers should be able to check-off a box on their internal revenue tax returns donating a part of their taxes to the National Endowment for the Arts, a system for raising and redistributing money similar to that adopted by Congress to help finance the 1976 national presidential campaigns. But that idea would take time to change for a proposal into law.

As Music Hall entered the last quarter of the 20th century, then, it and the neighborhood, city, and

metropolis of which it formed a part faced another crisis. Cincinnati boosters no longer plotted, as they had in the 19th century, to become one of three or four national metropolises, or even Queen City of the western, central and southern states. Instead, they struggled for socio-economic and amenities dominance in the tri-state metropolitan area, and in a region embracing the immediate hinterlands of Indianapolis, Dayton, Columbus, Charleston, West Virginia, Lexington, Nashville and Louisville. So far as national aspirations went, they took great satisfaction when the *Christian Science Monitor* and *Saturday Review* in 1976 named Cincinnati one of the nation's most livable cities, a laurel which the new center for the performing arts in Music Hall helped secure. But the glow faded fast, for in 1977 another "quality of life" evaluation in a book ironically called *Help* placed Cincinnati outside the country's top twenty cities, twenty-fourth on a list which placed San Francisco and Minneapolis at the top and New York City, Louisville and Columbus twenty-third, thirty-first, and thirty-third respectively. That same year, moreover, the *New York Times* reported the discomforting news that civic leaders in Louisville had embarked upon a performing arts effort to relieve that city's elite of the need to travel to New York or Los Angeles "to stay abreast of" symphonic music, ballet, opera, and theatre.

Worse still, no one anywhere seemed confident of possessing a clear definition of let alone a solution to the national contemporary metropolitan crisis. The perception of resource, energy, capital and tax revenue shortages exacerbated and reformulated the traditional competition among big city neighborhoods, between big cities and their suburbs, among townships, villages, and cities within metropolitan areas, among metropolitan areas within larger urban sub-regions, and between the frostbelt and the sunbelt. These conflicts, conducted in a win or lose atmosphere, inflicted a debilitating paralysis on the political process at the local, state, and national levels and diverted attention everywhere from the notion of the interdependence of territorial, racial, and ethnic groups and of the interrelatedness of economic, social, high culture, and popular leisure interests. In this milieu it seemed unlikely that Queensgate II, Music Hall, or the arts establishment, not to mention the city and other metropolitan area governments, could expect much in the way of federal assistance to ease their pressing problems.

It remained to be seen as the Music Hall Association prepared for its centennial celebration whether this generation of metropolitan leaders would be able to think and act anew on familiar problems, and to respond imaginatively, constructively, and humanely to novel and difficult conditions. But historical perspective offers encouragement. The past is past, and just as Music Hall, its neighborhood, city, and the metropolis of the late 19th century differed from those of the mid-20th century, so too will those of the late 20th century differ from those of the mid-20th century. What they will become depends on how this generation perceives and decides to solve its metropolitan problems.

But by 1977 the time was running short. Clearly, the acid of urban decay respected neither big city nor suburban neighborhood boundaries, a view re-inforced by the growing recognition that the much publicized return of the middle classes to old, rehabilitated big city neighborhoods most probably would be negated by the relocation of the dispossesed poor and lower-middle classes in the aging areas of the outer-city, the inner-suburbs, and the jerrybuilt ranch house developments from the 1950s and 1960s in the neighborhoods just beyond. Meanwhile, at the heart of the metropolis, the black ghetto simmered, building up frustrations and tensions deceptively veiled by a truce in racial conflict composed of relief among most whites at the passing of the militance and activism of the social justice movement of the 1960s and temporary discouragement and exhaustion among blacks stemming from the small gains which that massive effort produced. In the final analysis,

the fates of Music Hall, its neighborhood, the city and the metropolis remained inextricably intertwined. Any successful resolution of their particular difficulties awaited genuine acknowledgement and action upon that reality.

Modern ramps, rails and a porch shelter provides convenience but not compatibility with the architecture about them. Upper roof ornaments are noticeably missing. The free-standing position of the towers is visible in this view.

SECTION TWO
THE ARCHITECTURE

Introduction

James Biddle

In descriptive histories of American architecture of the 1800s and early 1900s, certain words are inescapable. Courthouses, city halls and other public buildings were "monumental." Churches were "inspiring." Theaters and auditoriums were "elegant."

Such terms are far removed from today's descriptions of most contemporary architecture, to which the words "functional" and "space efficient" are ubiquitously applied without regard to the structure's intended purpose. With few exceptions, these words seem to be the highest compliments our society pays to its newly-built environmental elements.

Newspaper accounts of building projects in the 19th century particularly were exuberant in their descriptions. And for good reason. In many cases, the local citizenry was involved in the project. The whole community had a stake in what was being constructed. From coast to coast, local pride in a community's new building gleamed through editorials declaring it "among the best in the nation."

This same community pride is evident in preservation projects that today are reviving the monumentality, inspiration and elegance of old buildings. While "functional, space efficient" office towers and shopping malls are put together by a handful of nearly invisible developers, engineers and contractors, it is usually enthusiastic local people of all ages and interests who co-operate to preserve their area's landmarks.

Such is the case with the Cincinnati Music Hall. It is and always has been the product of local efforts and the object of local pride. A Cincinnati architect designed it. Cincinnati craftsmen built and embellished it. Committees of Cincinnati residents guided its construction and operation. Costs were paid by Cincinnati money. And now Cincinnatians have worked hard to preserve and restore it to an active role in the community's cultural life.

But Music Hall has also been part of a greater national movement, both in its original construction and in its preservation. In the latter half of the 19th century, communities throughout the country were constructing great theaters and auditoriums. Regional and ethnic influences were strong; cities such as Cincinnati with large German-American populations put the cultural spotlight on music, and halls for choral singing sprang up. Whatever art form was most popular in a community, the theater was sure to employ the latest technological innovations in acoustics, lighting, mechanical systems and comfort. Age-old skills were combined with new ones in elaborate schemes of decoration and often wildly-creative design.

Many communities in the United States have allowed their theaters and performing arts halls to decay or be torn down. But others, like Cincinnati, have recognized the aesthetic, cultural and economic value of preserving the elegant public palaces of the past. The 1889 Auditorium Theater in Chicago, designed by the world-famous team of Adler and Sullivan, had been badly misused for 25 years until it was restored by the University of Chicago beginning in 1967. City officials, local industry, private philanthropy and the federal government co-operated to restore the Pabst Theater in Milwaukee (another city with strong German influences) in 1975, 80 years after it was built and six years after it had closed its doors for what many thought would be the last time. In East Haddam, Connecticut, the Goodspeed Opera House, built a century ago, was going to be torn down in 1958 to make room for a concrete garage to house state highway trucks. A local group organized to restore the building, and since 1963 its stage has been in constant use. The 1871 Grand Opera House in Wilmington, Delaware, has been the object of an ambitious restoration program and is once again a vital community center for the arts. Cincinnati was fortunate that, although its Music Hall fell on hard times in the 20th century, the building remained in use throughout its history.

What is behind this national fervor to preserve old arts centers? One factor, of course, is spiraling construction costs that make new performing arts centers exorbitantly expensive. But equally important is the realization that old theaters are often structurally sound, acoustically superb, visually appealing and easily adapted to meet modern needs. Cincinnati has capitalized on its artistic treasure in a way that makes other cities envious. The preserved Music Hall has been fitted with the most up-to-date theater equipment, while the architectural opulence of the 1870s has been richly restored.

The one feature that distinguished the Cincinnati Music Hall from similar buildings in other cities was its second purpose: in addition to giving pleasure to the many citizens who enjoyed music, its two flanking halls were large display areas for annual expositions of industrial progress. For years Horticulture Hall and Machinery Hall both reflected and stimulated the economy of the entire region. This unique combination of the arts and industry was an unexpected bonus in later years. As the importance of the two halls for exposition purposes declined in the early 20th century, the space within them was adapted for a variety of purposes. Thanks to this original design, the building still offers plenty of space for expansion of arts and related programs. The lack of such space too often forces other cities to abandon their old auditoriums and construct new arts centers.

Today the preservation of Cincinnati's great landmark continues to serve an economic as well as a cultural purpose. Large corporations are attracted to communities that have firm cultural foundations and ample artistic resources. The physical upgrading of old theaters and public buildings can be an impetus to other community revitalization. Houses in the residential neighborhoods near Music Hall are being rehabilitated, thus strengthening the tax base of the city. It may be difficult to determine to what extent the Music Hall restoration has influenced this trend, but certainly the two types of rehabilitation projects are mutually supportive.

This kind of revitalization — building by building, block by block — is happening in communities across the nation. The National Trust for Historic Preservation since 1949 has encouraged and assisted this kind of activity through publications, conferences, advice and grants. But always it is up to local residents, drawing on local pride, money and talent, to make preservation work. The same combination of private citizens, industry, foundations and city government that built the Cincinnati Music Hall in 1878 provided the winning formula for its preservation a century later. While the building has been given a new life, the pride and musical traditions of the city have also been restored. "Elegance" is back in Cincinnati.

James Biddle, President
National Trust for Historic Preservation
Washington, D. C.

The Building of Music Hall

George F. Roth, A. I. A.

S amuel Hannaford, architect and superintendant, designed the Cincinnati Music Hall and Exposition Center. The Hall was completed in 1878 in time for the Music Festival of that year and the Exposition Buildings were made ready for the Industrial Exposition of 1879.

This postwar era in the last quarter of the 19th century displayed in America a phase of architectural transition increasingly interesting to historians. It was a period of technical innovation with accompanying industrial clamor and labor's awakening. Invention and mechanization, new materials and methods, unplanned growth of cities and the introduction of disciplining building codes; new wealth, proud and ruthless wealth with ostentation over a sordid, social poverty — these things, in America as in Europe, demanded a new aesthetic of architect and craftsman.

Hannaford, as many other designers, must have experienced a groping for a genuine expression in the cultural tastes of this Victorian age. He was a contender in the architectural "battle of styles" which freckled the cities of the nation in their fervent growth. For this Music Hall and Exposition Center he chose, in the eclecticism of the time, to design an enveloping fabric which to some degree may be classified as "High Victorian Gothic;" expressing, as he must have seen it, the spirit of festivity. In this he is aesthetically related to Viollet-LeDuc, Augustus Pugin, and to Andrew Jackson Downing, Calvert Vaux, James Borgardus, Frank Furness of Philadelphia, Frederic Withers of New York and many others.

As a result, Cincinnati owns one of the best examples of this architectural vernacular, and the city has shown wisdom in maintaining both its character and its intended function, resisting efforts to replace it with a contemporary structure.

The program for the planning of Cincinnati's Music Hall and adjacent Exposition Center is not fully recorded, but the wishes of the main donor, Reuben Springer, were set in a brief letter by him and, likely, were reflected in instrucions given to the designers by the building committee, the members of which were Julius Dexter, William H. Harrison and Joseph Longworth. The new Music Hall should, Springer stated, be a "permanent structure and solely in the interests of the people and for public good." He did not visualize a luxurious palace. Rather, he set criteria that reflected careful consideration of cost; the building to accommodate 5000 spectators, but not a "fire-proof" structure, a method of construction far too expensive in Springer's judgment.

Controversy followed over unequal emphasis on musical presentations and industrial expositions. A "space committee" finally recorded the necessity of two great halls — one on the south of the central Music Hall to be a "Horticulture Hall" (later an Art Hall); the northern a "Power Hall" or "Machinery Hall." In these pavilions the industrial expositions were to be staged and planning for them required the in-put of the Chamber of Commerce, the Board of Trade and faculty of the Ohio Mechanics Institute. Where to locate the new structures was less of a problem, with the Saengerfest Hall site becoming available.

Firms from whom designs were requested, or by whom they were offered, included well known professional leaders, several having designed similar projects. Ware and VanBrunt of Boston, designers of the Boston Music Hall, were among the architects solicited. A review of the design presented by Ware and VanBrunt published in the American Architect and Building News of September 16, 1876, gives a clue to the requirements placed before the architects. The submitted design emphasized the separation of entry and exit to the auditorium level unencumbered by circulation to the first and second balconies, providing very wide staircases. For emergency evacuation, numerous exits were planned, with estimates that the entire building could be emptied in eight to ten minutes. With a capacity of 5109 persons, it is doubtful that evacuation in such short time could be accomplished even with the multiple means of egress. Gas jets for lighting and the installation of large ventilation shafts and towers are noted as features of interest. But most important is the presentation of size, shape and orientation of elements in the plan to accomplish optimum acoustical conditions, with seven major design criteria listed.

The firm of Alexander F. Oakey of New York presented a scheme, but the offering was not carried to the desired finish. Oakey's real contribution, however, was his counsel in design and materials selection for interior finishes to obtain optimum acoustical qualities.

In Cincinnati, four architects were consulted. One was a popular designer, James W. McLaughlin, who had designed a number of the city's outstanding buildings and was a favorite of John Shillito, a leading mercantile business man and civic benefactor. McLaughlin was a prime mover in the forming of the Cincinnati Chapter of

† SAM'L HANNAFORD.   J. W. McLAUGHLIN   † HENRY BEVIS.

S. W. ROGERS   † A C. NASH   † J. K WILSON   † E. ANDERSON   AUTHER BATES

CHARTER MEMBERS OF CIN. CHARTER A. I. A. 1870.

The architects in this picture were called together by Mr.
James W. McLaughlin early in 1870 to form the Cincinnati
Chapter of the American Institute of Architects. McLaughlin,
in mid-position, points a pencil to the drawing before them
while Samuel Hannaford, the designer of Music Hall, is
standing second from the left.

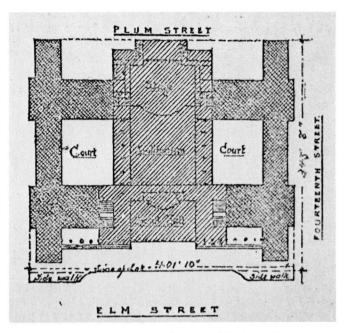

Taken from the American Architect and Building News, September, 1876, this plan is the submittal of the firm of Ware and Van Brunt of Boston.

the American Institute of Architects in 1870, the fourth in the nation. Hannaford, born in Devonshire, England, had become a Cincinnatian in his early youth. He worked in the local offices of J. H. Hamilton and others and had grown in professional stature and repute as a result of his exciting design productions. There were William Walter, creator of the great Cincinnati classic church, St. Peter in Chains, and Henry Proctor, an associate of Hannaford. Julius Dexter, as chairman of the building committee, traveled to Philadelphia, New York and Boston to inspect buildings of similar purpose. Submitted designs were not widely different in general concept, all of them tri-pavilion plans but including courts and varied circulation patterns.

After review and study of the suggested plans, the contract for the commission was signed with Hannaford and Proctor; the site acquired from the city with reluctant action of the officials on April 3, 1876, and the old Saengerfest Hall buildings sold to the newly formed Music Hall Association for $2105. The architects were urged to bring their planning to completion for approval as quickly as possible, hoping for construction completion in time for the 1878 Music Festival. The publicized announcement of the selection of architects for the project listed dimensions of the buildings, both horizontal and vertical, and the capacity of 6500 including audience, chorus and orchestra.

The description of the design presented in the American Architect and Building News of April, 1878, presumably by Hannaford, is factual and detailed.

"The Elm Street facade of the Hall is 182' wide and 150' high, to the apex of the central gable. From a flagged pavement 40' wide a flight of steps leads to a stone terrace 12' wide, on which open nine vestibules 15' x 7'-3", of which the entrances are 11' wide, affording a clear entrance way of 99'. The grand vestibule is 46' x 112', and is 42' high, with a broad balcony at the level of the gallery in the hall; and the north and south vestibules measure 31' x 46' and are 20' high. From these vestibules solid

stone stairways 12'-8" wide lead to the galleries and upper rooms. The auditorium of Music Hall proper is 112' wide, 192' long and 64' high. The stage is 112' x 56', the organ, however, intrudes upon this space by occupying an area about 15' x 50'. Accommodation is afforded for a chorus of 686 singers and an orchestra of 100 performers. The floor of the auditorium rises from the stage to the entrance 4'-8", the stage level being at its front 4'-4" above the floor, with a rise of 14 inches from front to rear. Three entrance doors, each 10' wide, lead from the grand vestibule to the Hall, while corridors 18' wide, with eight doors each 7' wide, give access to the hall on the sides, thus giving a total of 86' in door-ways. Separate doors lead to the stage. The corridors extend through the building and communicate with Plum Street. A flight of stone steps 9' wide, in each corridor, leads to the upper stories. In emptying the house, cross-currents will be avoided. Back of the stage are retiring-rooms for the performers, while water-closets and wash-rooms are amply provided under the several flights of stairs.

"An examination of the dimensions of the auditorium, before given, will show that a unit of 16' has been used. A gallery 16' wide extends around three sides of the hall at the second floor level, while an upper gallery of like width extends across the end opposite the stage. The Hall gives promise of being an acoustic success, having been used on two occasions for mass rehearsals for the Festival Chorus; the full proof, however, of this vitally important matter is still to come on the occasion of the opening. In the second and third stories over the several vestibules are rooms for the use of conventions and other large gatherings. Over the grand vestibule in the third story is a small hall, 46' x 112'. It will probably be called Dexter Hall, after Julius Dexter, a liberal subscriber to the building fund, secretary of the board of trustees, and chairman of the building committee. Dexter Hall is approached by two easy flights of stone stairs, each 7' wide. The Elm Street facade is built of pressed brick, ornamented with black brick in the arches, etc., and relieved with bands and moulded string courses of Ohio River sandstone. The bricks are laid in black mortar, with a sunken joint, 8/16" deep. The effect is to give a decided structural appearance to the surface, which in so large a building is an advantage. The Plum Street facade is built of best quality common red brick laid in yellow mortar with flush joints. The effect is to enhance greatly the body color of the building; so that in the glow of an afternoon sun it warms to the intensity of coral.

"The entire length of the building is 303'-4" The total number of rooms is 37, exclusive of the Main Hall and Dexter Hall. The walls and ceiling of the Main Hall are lined with wood, — no plastering being used. Under the system of seating adopted for the coming Musical Festival the Hall will accommodate an audience of 4428."

The three "halls" were completed at a cost of $496,943.78, exclusive of the great organ. Of this sum, $296,050.62 was expended in the construction and equipment of central Music Hall.

Perhaps the fact that the earlier Saengerfest Hall had tower motifs at the four corners inspired Hannaford to create a reminiscence, with the two eastern towers capped by heavily corbelled arches and sharply conicle roofs. The great hall was, obviously, intended to be expressed in the east facade by the wide, pointed brick arch with a large circular window approximately 30 feet in diameter with

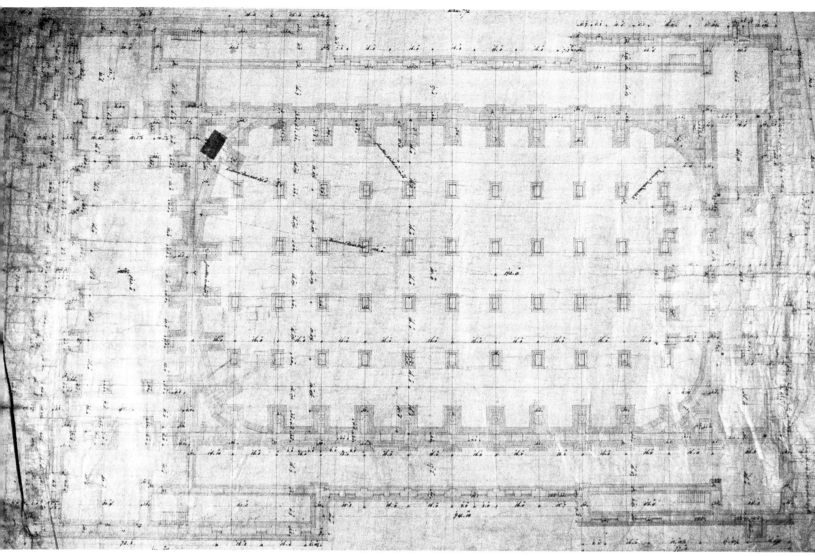

This badly scarred tracing — an inked drawing on
transparent linen cloth — shows the foundation pattern of the
initial 1877 construction.

This original plan of the third level of
the three building units shows the very
limited gallery and Dexter Hall.
Through the reception room one could
pass to the North Hall, and on the
south the ''dressing room'' gave access
to exhibition space and stairs in
Horticultural Hall.

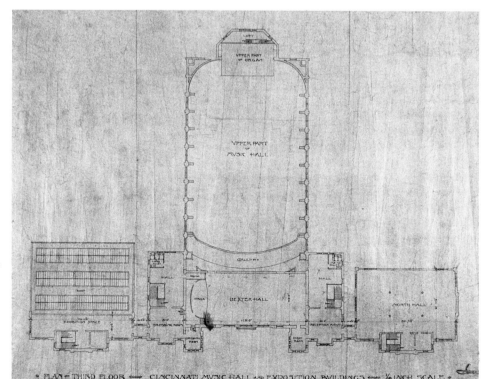

63

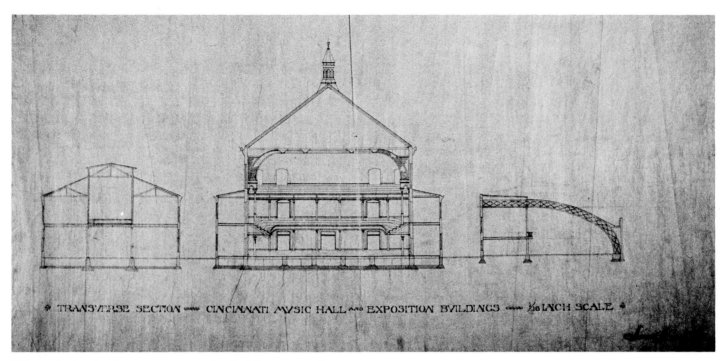

This early drawing is a transverse section looking eastward showing the balcony and limited upper gallery. Of interest here is the form originally designed as roof structure for Horticultural Hall (right) which was to have an iron, arched roof truss with skylight.

three glazed arches below. The two great towers, free standing above the lower story, serve to visually contain the gabled facade and to arrest the apparent thrust of the arch.

A variety of ceramic shapes and colors appears in the intricate masonry work. The base material is brick; machine pressed brick laid with small, tight joints, raked deeply. It is said that masons from the eastern states were called to do this finish work while local masons constructed the brick and stone structural masses. The facades are woven together by numerous horizontal stone belt courses. The various types of arches, corbels, ornate label moulds, denticular courses, balconies, balustrades and copings create a "fabrique" in which bright red and black brick, stone, slate and tile combine in a craftsman's delight. The great roof surfaces, high pitched and very visible, were carefully designed to include red and grey slate in horizontal stripes and serrated panels. And to decorate and sharpen the ridges and apexes of the roofs, iron finials, crestings, ventilating lanterns and flag poles were added, with little worry over the problems of raising and lowering the flags. The flanking exposition buildings, originally separated by carriage lanes between them and the hall, display similar architectonic appointments but with less variety and exuberance. Architecturally these northern and southern buildings seem to be separated from the great central mass by narrow pavilions, their facades including projecting bays supported by masonry brackets growing from a single brick pier. All three, the great hall and the north and south structures, are now joined, and the original carriage lanes long since closed in various building remodeling and expansion programs.

Beyond the eastern section of the building mass, the portion which sheltered the auditorium area is basically a simple structure. The chorus and orchestra area, which initially was a loft in the great hall, has become a stage for dramatic and opera productions with proscenium and supporting equipment. The western facade, which was at times visible from the canal and Lincoln Park, is less exciting but reveals in the masses and forms the space utilization of the interior. The brick is of a less refined type, although the corbelled arch motif at the roof line is retained. Additions of entrance shelters and the recent bridge approach have been rendered in compatible materials.

The original slate has given way to modern asphalt composition shingle which retains somewhat the original pattern and approximates the color. Metal roof ornaments, so carefully detailed in early drawings, have disapppeared. A crowning, winged goddess figure shown at the point of the east gable never was installed.

The architect's drawings, inked on tracing cloth, are only partially available, although some hundred sheets have been placed in the archives of the Cincinnati Historical Society by Thomas Landise, an architect who, having acquired the remnants of the Hannaford firm's files, recognized their importance. One remaining well-preserved drawing of the east facade served as the guide for the masons, and displays the intricate dimensioning systems employed to clarify the complex brick work. It reveals the architect's technique of graphically imparting his design details to the craftsmen.*

Between the rendering and presentation of a design for an edifice and the production of the final building, many of the artistic appointments included by the delineator are often lost. But comparison of the remaining drawings of the Music Hall, photographs taken at various times in the colorful history of the place and the present building, displays that there was a remarkable completion in most details, even to the smaller of the iron finials at the points of the dormers, gables and towers. The facades are replete with many architectural motifs, difficult of fabrication and construction.

A display of masonry intricacies indicates the superb craftsmanship required to construct the architect's carefully delineated motifs of his design for the main facade. Note the date stone designating 1877 as a construction date. The completed building was opened for the Music Festival of the spring of 1878.

Detail drawing showing original wood paneling of walls. The location of peripheral columns in the 1876 design is seen in the section on the right.

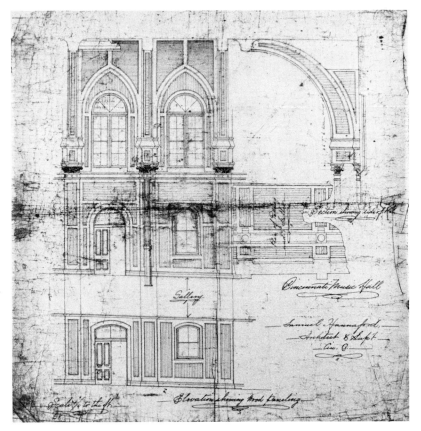

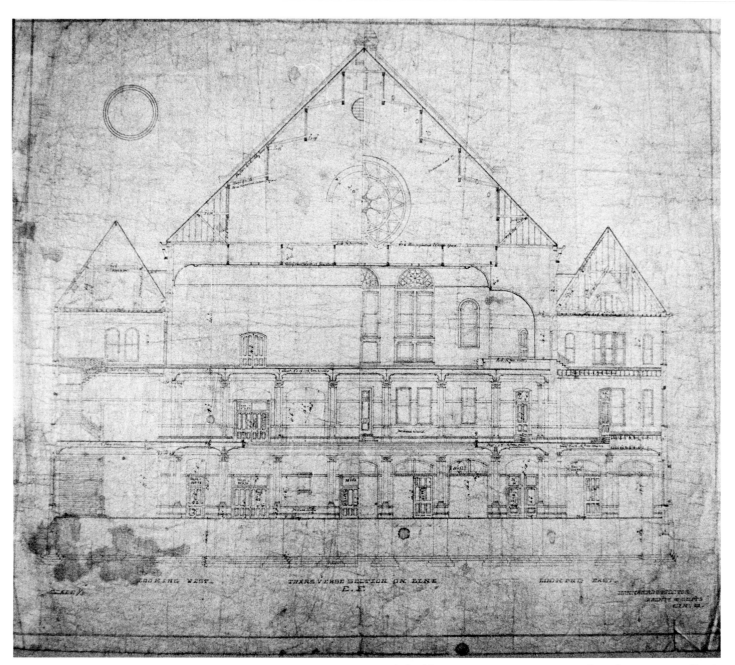

A double transverse section is cut to show the interior walls of the lobby, balcony and Dexter Hall, the smaller auditorium. The views are both to the east, with the original great windows of Dexter Hall and the circular window in the gable, as well as the west walls of the three levels. The drawing is of 1876.

*It is this drawing which is reproduced on the dust jacket of this book.

The total concept is, however, an architectural festivity, an expression of the overwhelming desire of the citizenry for a great cultural center — a festival hall. It was a work of pride, a production demanded by the cultural and industrial enterprise of a nervously energetic community, and the architect, it seems, succeeded in designing a surprising building that reflected the joyfulness of the people — "The voice of the people speaking in their building" and singing, too. The Zeitgeist of Cincinnati.

Paraphrasing a Robert Frost expression, one must have "a lover's quarrel" with this vast structure. It seems over-wrought, overly eclectic, energetically picturesque; yet very "human," very exciting. Inconsistently grand in scale and dimension, yet entertaining, it does the job inside and out. Montgomery Schyler, famed critic observed in 1908 — "it is a real composition and it is highly commendable for its comparative quietude in a style in which . . . keeping quiet was the most difficult thing for a designer to do."

Even as the builders were pushing construction, suggestions for changes in the design were presented. Nineteenth century "change orders" were issued from the start of operations. An examination of the remaining drawings and miscellaneous design sketches reveals an almost continuous interest in altering sections of the complex to accommodate varied functions.

The success of the 1878 opening music festival and the industrial exhibitions of the following years arranged in the exposition halls brought a desire to increase the seating capacity of the great auditorium. Many studies of

Corbelled brick arches of the great gable, the complex brick label motif and dentil course ornamenting the grand gothic arch, the wood tracery of the circular window, stone finials and coping, multi-color brick pattern — all are woven into a vibrant architectural assembly.

seating arrangements are to be seen in the preserved drawings. Remaining, also, are concepts for an iron structure spanning the width of the southern hall, which was prepared for exhibits of horticulture although the pavilion was designated to provide displays of the arts generally. Development of parks and extensive landscaped gardens related to the large country seats of influential Cincinnati families of this romantic era was a proud concern. Horticulture Hall was designed as a two-story building, the second level as a great greenhouse with gracefully arched trusses swung overhead and oriented to the south to support the glass panels through which the southern light would be received. This design was never executed. The present iron truss structure, although with a bowed lower chord, symmetrically supports the roof which may have included skylights.

The northern hall was intended to provide space for the display and operation of machinery in a manner not unlike the Machinery Hall of the Arts and Industries Museum of the Smithsonian Institution in Washington, D. C. , a museum not dedicated and opened to the public until 1881. For this, a steam boiler plant was installed to drive the power shafts to which the machines were connected by belts. The smoke from the coal-fired boiler was considered of less environmental disturbance if emitted on the northern side of the complex, prevailing winds out of the south-west.

The construction of Music Hall was "fast-tracked." Before the drawings were off the drafting board, demolition of the old Halle, clearing of the site (which unearthed numerous graves requiring re-internment in Spring Grove Cemetery), and the excavation and foundation work was started. This was in October of 1876. Henry Proctor, superintendant, and John MacCammon,

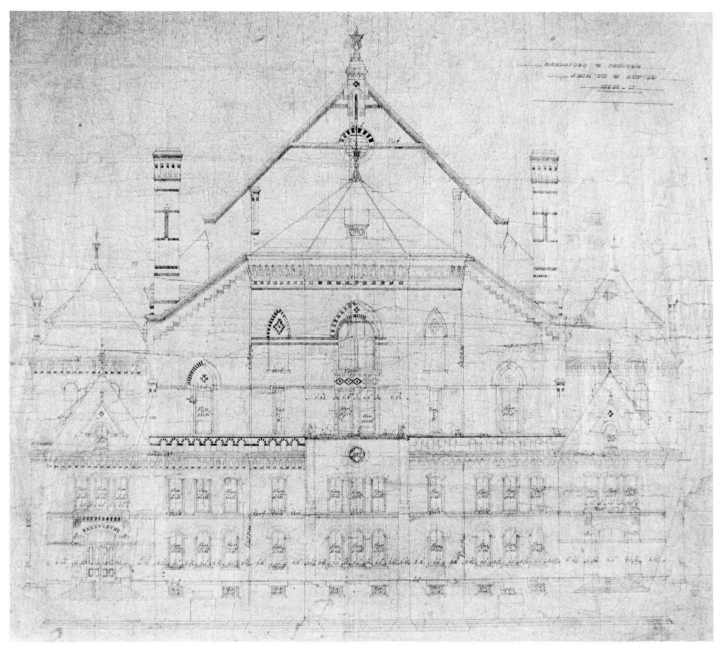

This 1876 drawing shows the rear or west facades which were to be seen from the canal. The authorship is noted as Hannaford & Procter, Arch'ts & Sup'td., Cin. O.

clerk of the works, were in charge. A very cold, early winter stopped construction of the concrete and limestone foundations in late December. When work was resumed in the spring of 1877, the mortar and concrete were found to have suffered deterioration, necessitating reconstruction of work which had been almost two-thirds completed. The resulting claims and placing of blame were, somehow, resolved.

The foundations are of large stone and concrete sections, with widely spread footings stepped to receive stone and brick masonry piers and walls. The masonry work is well executed and still in good condition. Above, and supported by the masonry understructure, the floor framing is of heavy wood beams, joists and sub-floors. Springer's counsel, nullifying the design of what was then considered fire-proof construction, was adopted, but the structural members in many areas have, over the succeeding years, been fire-protected by the application of metal lath and plaster envelope. The wood beams are

assisted by heavy iron flitch plates and staggered through-bolting, joining two four by sixteen inch wood sections. Short span-structure supports the heavy marble floor of the great lobby and the wide stairs, which are constructed of stone treads and cast-iron frames with rails of Italianate square newels and balustrades. In the basement, the positions of brick piers and related foundation walls reveal the locations of the cast-iron columns above and the intially curved walls enclosing the auditorium. The cast-iron columns continue through the superstructure to support the balcony and the gallery, these latter expanded in succeding remodeling programs.

Ventilation of the auditorium was accomplished by the insertion of numerous floor apertures through which it was intended that the "foul" air would pass to two large ducts, which, in turn, connected to shafts in the corners of the hall where the curved interior walls provided large triangular flues open to the roof area.

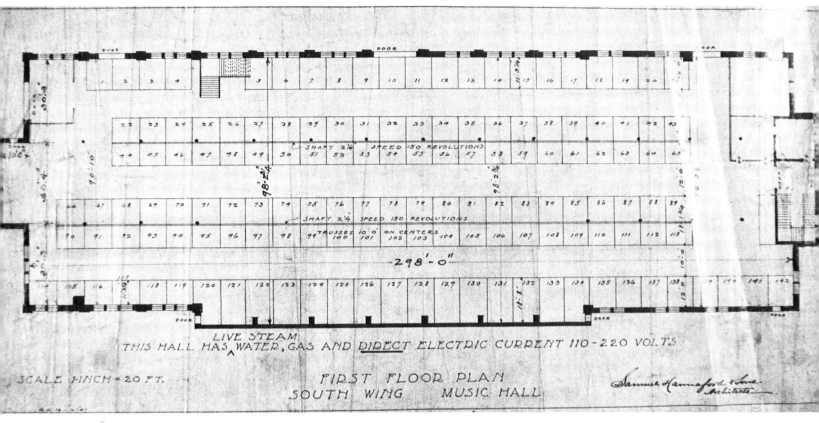

This drawing carries a date of 1887 showing a plan for exhibits in Power Hall or Machinery Hall. Two shafts of 2¼" dimension at 150 revolutions are noted to be powered by "live" steam. Water, gas and electric current of 110-220 volts were supplied. The North wing or hall, rather than the South wing, was used for this purpose.

The interior design of the initial construction of 1876-78 was truly a great hall conceived as a large shell in which musical programs of considerable magnitude could be presented. Although the early descriptions refer to a stage, the reference is to the western elevated portion of the floor upon which the great organ occupied the central position, flanked by curved banks of seats to accommodate the numerous members of the choruses. The orchestra was located directly in front of the pipe organ. There was no proscenium, no curtain.

A theory of the acoustical engineers and scientists of the time, including A. F. Oakey, was that the longitudinal section of the hall should locate the seating of the musicians and chorus elevated in a vertically curved bank with a large cove above, extending into the ceiling over the listeners, and the rows of seats of the "parquet" floor should rise in a continuous parabolic curve to a height close to the cove of the ceiling at the opposite end of the hall. The subtlety of the curvature of the back and belly of a violin was cited as possible optimum form for faithful sound production and migration.

The interior of this great curved shell was entirely of wood — thin pine wood, oiled on the wall surfaces and with varnish applied to the ceiling only. Above the gallery level, the north and south side walls contained ten stained glass windows.

The roof structure over the Auditorium is a vast array of iron forms assembled as great trusses, all compression members of which are doubled 8-inch channels held in bowed separation by iron castings, but united where connections with the "eyes" of the large diameter tension rods occur. The top chord of this unusual truss is supported by a central compression column and two lesser interior trusses constructed similarly but of smaller members. These frames are placed at 16-foot intervals, a module noted in early accounts of acoustical phenomena as optimum for sound-wave dimensions. But direct relation of truss position to interior ceiling design is no longer evident. In the mid area of this complicated array of wood and iron structural members, a cabinet approximately ten feet square houses the remains of the very early "echo" organ, an adjunct element of the great central instrument.

The structure sheltering the eastern frontal section of the building, that area where the original Dexter Hall was located and extending to greater height than the auditorium roof, is separated from the great hall by a formidable brick wall with a wide arch in the central position. This handsome masonry motif is in axis with the large circular wood-traceried window of the eastern facade. The original Dexter Hall ceiling was located 21 feet above the floor and the framed support system remains. The roof structure is entirely of wood members in this eastern, highest element of the building.

At this writing the introduction into this loft space of large metal ducts, conduit for lighting, the motorized mechanism for lowering and raising the great crystal chandelier, smoke detection and sprinkler system piping entwines and mixes in the curious spectacle of 19th century, admirable craftsmanship and building methods to create a roof form enveloping a great volume of architectonic space, a design technique not condoned in the contemporary economic disciplines of space utilization.

69

A view of the central, bowed compression member of the "Fink" truss, and the trussed top cord upon which the roof framing rests. The brick wall is the upper portion of the proscenium separation of the auditorium and stage. The entire roof space is protected by a sprinkler system.

From the gridiron above the auditorium ceiling, one can examine the bowed compression members and the ceiling supporting suspension rods of the iron trusses.

Shown here is the original timber of the roof construction at the eastern end behind the great central gable. This structure sheltered the original Dexter Hall, now redesigned and called Corbett Tower.

In 1883, four years after completion of the complex, at the death of Joseph Longworth, first president of the Music Hall Association, an adjacent structure for the new College of Music was considered requiring remodeling of the southern exterior walls. Reuben Springer, who died in June of 1884, left a considerable sum to assure continued maintenance of the structures and their cultural programs. But demands for use of the facilities pressed heavy decisions upon the controlling board. Established rental conditions prohibited use of the buildings for "theatrical or dramatic performances, equestrian or circus performances, sparring exhibitions and variety shows. No selling or giving away of ale, beer, porter or spiritous liquors . . ." But in 1880, on the occasion of the formal opening of the Cincinnati Southern Railroad between Cincinnati and Chattanooga, Tennessee, 2000 guests were served at one sitting at a banquet which included four wines. This ceremony, arranged by Edward Roth of the St. Nicholas Hotel, was staged in the great, new Music Hall.

In 1890, a riding school was granted permission to use the entire first floor of Music Hall. The horses were, of necessity, housed elsewhere.

It was in 1894 that the board agreed to remodel to accommodate theatrical and opera troupes, and this decision brought about the major revision which is evident today. Samuel Hannaford and Sons were, again, employed to design the alterations to the auditorium at a total cost of $120,000, all raised by public subscription.

The stage area was extended, the organ moved back 12 feet, and a proscenium wall and arch were constructed. Equipment for stage productions was installed.

The wood wall lining and ceilings were removed and the entire interior re-designed with "plaster surfaces and decoration."

The floor pitch was changed, although there remained a lower level floor which could be exposed and used for "large balls," exhibitions and conventions. A new seating arrangement was designed and upholstered seats were purchased to accommodate 4200-seated spectators. A new system of electric lighting, heating and ventilating apparatus was installed.

Changes were made in the entrances and exits, with ticket offices relocated.

As would be expected, much interest was manifest in the design and appointments of the new stage where none existed previously, and when completed, it was pronounced one of the finest in the nation. The original width of 112 feet was retained but the depth from the new curtain line became 54 feet. Adding the forward extension, the total depth of the stage floor grew to 70 feet, sufficiently large for great theatrical spectacles and choruses. The proscenium was planned to be double to provide dimensional flexibility; the established opening of 72 feet was to be reduced to 50 feet by hydraulically moved side wings traveling on a radial track. This scheme was not carried to completion although detailed drawings were prepared for it by Hannaford with Thomas G. Smith, Jr. as mechanical engineer. Dressing rooms were on two levels, and an hydraulic lift was provided to move the performers' baggage to the upper rooms.

The proscenium arch was decorated by John Rettig, a prominent local artist and designer of many festival settings and spectacles, some of which displayed ingenious planning and artistry.

With removal of the original pine walls and ceiling work, and reshaping of the entire auditorium to accommodate the stage and orchestra area, there were also major revisions in the design of the balcony and gallery as well as the segregated boxes. Cast iron columns were re-located to support new structural systems. Upper windows were permanently closed and wall surfaces redesigned to include wainscots with wood paneling. The bellied balcony facia was decorated with palmetto motifs. The ceiling became a complex, large-scale pattern of deep coffers between beams, the coffers containing large folliated rosettes surrounded by classic moulds.

The central ceiling area is composed of a shallow saucer dome, the curved surface of which displays a mural depicting an "Allegory of the Arts." The earlier intent was that the painting decorate the wall above the proscenium arch. This colorful work was executed by Arthur Conrad Thomas in 1905 at a time when the great aerial ceilings of Tiepolo, the Italian master of the Rennaisance era, and the Baroque church work in Germany were studied in American schools. The oil painting was coated with a parafin wax to protect it against the deposits of air-borne soil and smudge rising from light

Shown here is an original circular wood frame of an early ceiling rondelle above the auditorium.

This is a partial view of the silhouetted tracery of the circular "wheel" or "Rose" window from inside. The frame is wood, heavily constructed to withstand wind pressures.

fixtures, heating devices, smoking tobacco and air-polluting matters of the era.

Thomas, the muralist, was born in Dresden, Germany, in 1858, and studied at the Royal Academy of Dresden under Heinrich Hofmann. He came to America in 1892. Records indicate that he completed allegorical and historic murals in the St. Louis City Hall, several courthouses in Indiana, and Louisville, Kentucky. He was commissioned to execute the Music Hall mural through the efforts of the decorator, William Frederick Behrens, and labored for several months on a scaffolding 73 feet above the auditorium floor. The figures, in rich color against a turbulent background, are grouped at the outer rim of the dome in the four representations of Music, Science, History, and Literature.

The opening of the stage brings the splayed proscenium arch to a rectangular shape. The great arch, however, is covered by a myriad of small coffers, each containing rosettes varying in dimension to fit the splayed and curved surface. Flanking panels, along with the stage-entrances over-door panels, are decorated as latticed with flowered rosettes in each aperture and surrounded by rope moulds, bulging cartouches and festoons of leaf forms about shells and harps.

*Bearing a date of October, 1895, this main floor plan shows
the very extensive remodeling executed at that time. The re-
located structural cast-iron columns support increased first
and second balconies which carry about the auditorium to the
newly introduced proscenium motif.*

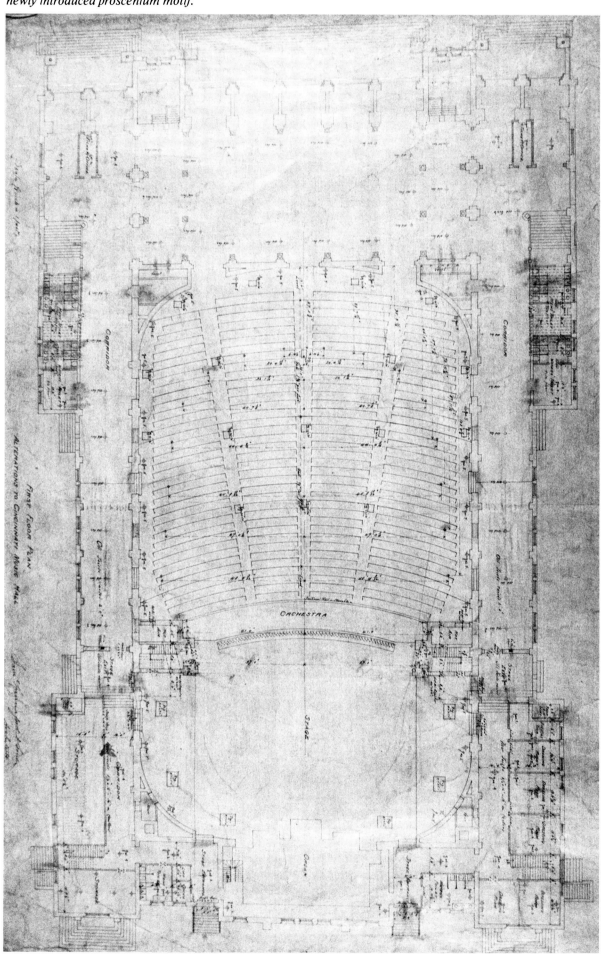

This is the 1895 remodeling plan for the second floor (lobby, balcony level) which remains at the present time. The original form about the stage was altered to accommodate the extensive modern equipment.

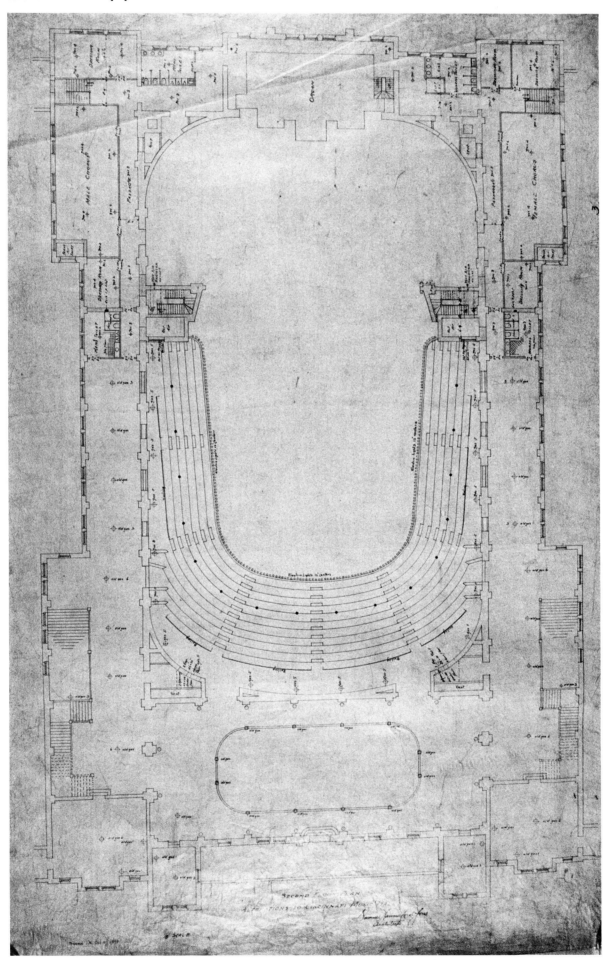

The newly re-created Music Hall was re-opened in May of 1896, and studies for modernization throughout the buildings seem to have continued thereafter. In 1900, a large Charity Ball required the leveling of the auditorium floor, and the newly instituted Fall Festivals of 1901, 1902, 1903 and 1906 required altered seating and exhibition arrangements. In 1909, the western entrances from Plum Street received considerable attention, and an iron and glass canopy, extending from the Horticulture Hall across the entire facade to the entrance of the original Power Hall on the north, was designed but not constructed. A drawing prepared in December of 1907 notes that the northern wing was prepared with direct electric current for 110-220 volts and water, gas and live steam. In 1913, the proscenium arch of the stage was again re-designed with new structural supports. The drawings exhibit, also, an extensive plan designed to accommmodate a very large religious convention utilizing and connecting all three buildings.

The First World War inflicted great trauma upon the people of the Cincinnati area. The joy of the musical programs disappeared, as did the efforts to maintain the Hall and the Exposition buildings. For some time another auditorium was used for symphony orchestra concerts.

In 1927, however, a very energetic Board of Trustees, with A. Clifford Shinkle as president and Robert A. Taft as vice president, prepared for the Golden Jubilee of Music Hall. Apparently hoping to generate new interest and uses for the buildings, they initiated a program of modernization of the northern and southern halls and planned a Greater Cincinnati Industrial Exposition. For this project, which cost $750,000, the architectural firm of Kruckemeyer and Strong was employed, with mechanical and electrical engineering designed by Fosdick and Hilmer, all of Cincinnati. The north wing was altered to accommodate boxing, wrestling, and other athletic programs. The two-level southern building was strengthened to house exhibitions, automobile shows and large social functions.

The canal was drained and in the channel the tubes for a rapid transit subway were constructed; the parkway boulevard over this area was to facilitate vehicular approach and increase attendance of functions staged in the exhibition buildings.

But this revivification was immediately tempered by the great economic depression of the '30s and the following years of war, during which maintenance of the entire complex fell to an appalling state of inadequacy. In the post-war years the mustiness, poor illumination and out-moded appointments of the interiors grew more and more depressing.

The originally designed Dexter Hall, high in the great eastern gable, was in disuse and had been for many years when in 1954 a "new idea" was permitted to locate in the large space. Education television had come to Cincinnati under the guidance of Umberto Neely, who as director of the adjacent College of Music, pioneered the establishment of a radio-television department. "Live" school programs were prepared in this upper room, and an innovative operation known as the Midwestern Project for Airborn Televised Instruction collaborated with Purdue University to deliver educational programs to schools throughout a wide region. Eventually the Cincinnati station became a member of the National

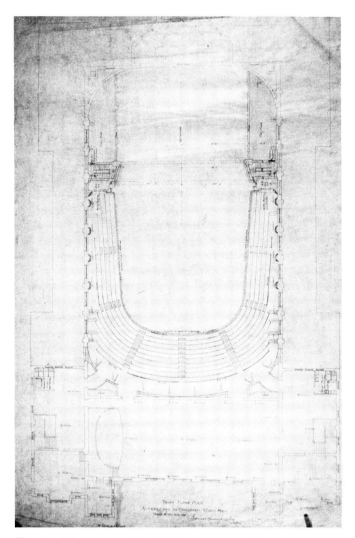

The third floor plan of the 1895 remodeling. The construction of the entire second balcony (or gallery) is shown. Dexter Hall remains on this plan unchanged. The area has become Corbett Tower in recent years.

Educational Television network and is now known as WCET-TV. Neely's vision of the immense impact of public television on the graphic and performing arts, as well as on educational processes, developed a fortunate phase of Cincinnati's cultural history.

In 1953, the record shows, a new tone of pride in the great structure lead to a minor face-lifting. This effort of renovation was not far reaching and included as a major element some new seating and repair. The great organ stood sentinel as it was placed in 1895 but not often played. The ceiling mural, so covered by soil, remained almost unseen. However, the acoustical qualities of the auditorium were admired in musical circles throughout the nation and symphony concerts and May Music Festivals were highly praised.

Expressed desires for a new, municipal exposition center and convention hall noted how inadequate were the facilities in the old complex on Elm Street. The architectural character of the buildings was degraded; public taste sought a new, fresh, functional facility, sufficiently large for modern conventions and displays of magnitude commensurate with the great scale and character of fast-growing American civic centers. So Cincinnati determined to erect a new convention center which could relate to central downtown activities.

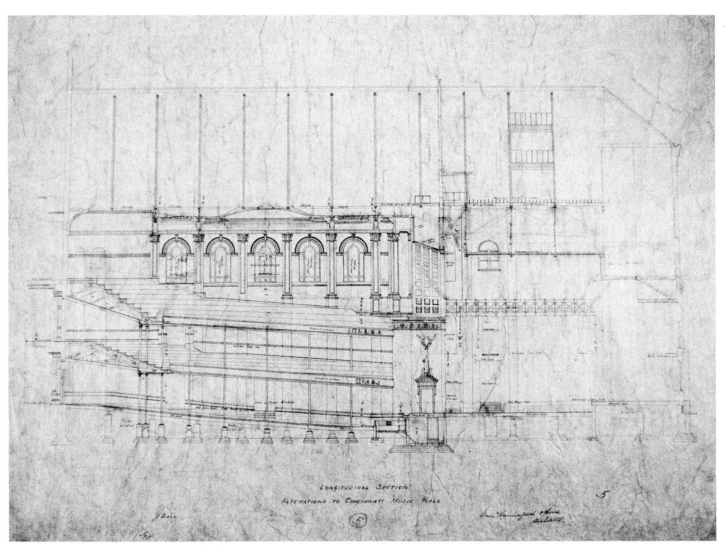

This longitudinal section shows the 1895 reconstruction of the auditorium and stage. Note the column system to support the first and second balconies.

As for Music Hall, the voices of dissatisfaction grew more numerous and demanding upon city officials to remove the great, old structures and to build a modern center for the performing arts.

However, in 1934, Cincinnati had welcomed Ralph and Patricia Corbett who had come from New York where both had interests in the cultural arts programs. They attended the performances in Music Hall and came to develop a great love for the "curious" old building, but noted, with some measure of depression, the low ebb of support for cultural pursuits in their new Midwestern environment. When, after considerable coercion, the city concluded that it would renovate rather than build anew, Corbett found himself chairman of the important committee representing the several local cultural organizations that would aid in the new effort of building restoration and program rejuvenation. His enthusiasm for making Music Hall one of the largest, best equipped and acoustically superior concert halls in the world has resulted thus far in 1977 in an expenditure of well over $12 million since the 1968 decision was reached at City Hall. The program of physical updating still continues, and a current verve of activity augurs well for more and continued care for the great structure.

To finance the new restoration, the city appropriated $3,077,100; the Cincinnati Symphony Orchestra contributed $800,000 and the Music Hall Association another $800,000. Dedicated citizens contributed in a way which recalls the 19th century civic enthusiasm for the initial building of the "Springer Music Hall." But the greatest financial energizing came from the new Corbett Foundation which chose to designate the Music Hall renovation one of its major projects and allocated grants totaling $5,515,500 to the work, with subsequent assignments that have brought increasing enrichment of the entire cultural center.

With the restoration program, the north and south wings could be brought to use for supportive facilities directly related to the central Music Hall. This space was, therefore, incorporated into the architectural plans and provided the growth areas so essential for the planned increase of programs that now include not only the Symphony Orchestra and May Festival choral presentations but also opera and ballet in large scale — and even an annual Saengerfest.

The wood flooring of the auditorium was repaired and in large measure replaced to receive new seats in a newly dimensioned arrangement, the total accommodations numbering 3631, including the balcony and gallery which also were renovated. Sightlines were greatly improved. Carpet was applied to the aisles of all three levels in color harmony with the new white, red, and gold interior. The

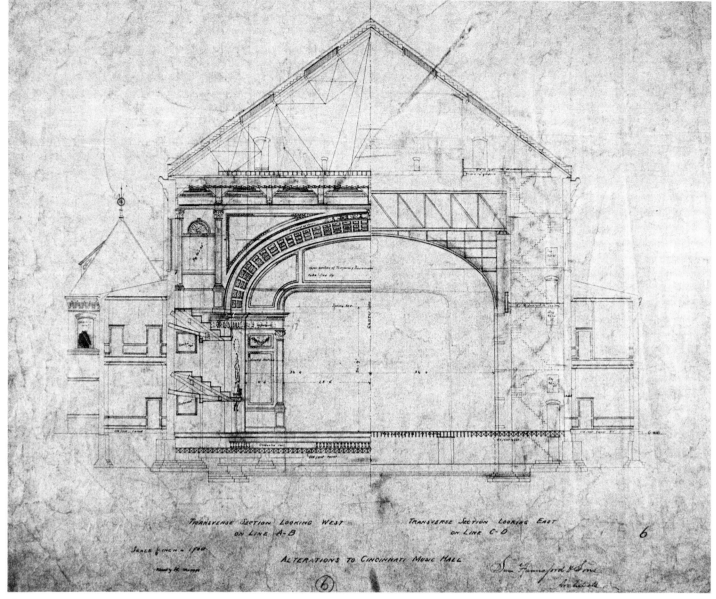

Transverse section through the auditorium showing the 1895 design of the proscenium arch and the roof trusses in diagram.

12 boxes above the parquet level were refurbished. The crystaline brightness of the new lighting design, which incorporates cciling and wall fixtures as well as powerful "down" lighting from the deep coffers high above, is dominated by a great chandelier which hangs from the roof structure and is stemmed through a rondelle grill in the center of the ceiling mural. The entire fixture, weighing approximately 1500 pounds and 20 feet in diameter, is elevated and lowered by motorized mechanism, supported in the original iron structure above and controlled from the stage equipment. This great chandelier was designed by George and Allan Schatz, architects for the restoration.

On-stage, many modernizations were effected, involving extensive structural changes to accommodate mechanical and electrical equipment. The new equipment includes a completely modern "memory board" Kliegl lighting system, one of the few of such size and complexity in the nation. From this board the lighting of the house, stage and bridge is governed. The bridge, constructed across the rear of the auditorium, controls frontal lighting totaling 120,000 watts. Above the stage, a 90-ton steel grid was added to support stage scenery and lighting lines,

and the old hemp and weight apparatus was replaced by an electrically operated counter-weight system. The fore-stage, extending in front of the house curtain and under the proscenium arch, 65 feet long and 19 feet wide, can now be lowered to a depth of nine feet to provide an orchestra pit for 80 musicians. And an electronic sound system has been designed to provide amplification for the most complicated, contemporary electronic music.

But the great organ, once occupying the focal center of the back stage, has been removed. The stage area has thus been increased and space provided for the numerous, ever-changing devices, props and equipment.

Backstage areas extending into the north and south buildings have been planned to include ensemble rehearsal space and a very versatile, second level, sound-proof chorus and small orchestra rehearsal room in which recordings are prepared. Ingenious planning permits this upper area to be divided also for dressing-room spaces. Another, almost stage-size rehearsal hall has been constructed in dimension sufficient for a full orchestra and the rehearsals of opera. Separate entrances to these facilities are incorporated.

3/4 SCALE DRAWING OF ORNAMENTAL PLASTER WORK
ALTERATIONS TO MUSIC HALL CINCINNATI, O.
SECTION THROUGH STAGE
SEPT. 95

SECTION THROUGH ORCHESTRA RAIL AND PIT

Elevation of Rail and Plan
Showing manner of Joining

*A detail drawing of some intended ornamental plaster work at
the fore stage and the facia of the balcony. Some of these
motifs were not installed.*

A vast, fully equipped two-level scenery storage area and a carpentry and prop construction shop has been built into the north pavilion which once served for industrial expositions.

The southern pavilion, once the "Horticulture" and "Arts" Hall, has been completely redesigned to provide offices for the numerous departments of administration, general offices, ticket and subscription processing, costume preparation and storage rooms, offices for the Symphony Orchestra, Opera, the May Festival, and Ballet. The Music Hall Association now has a meeting place. Backstage on this southern side are five close-to-stage dressing rooms, a stage crew room and a music library, with conductor's and concertmaster's offices. The "Green Room" in a central position in the artists' backstage area, has five dressing rooms in close proximity and a suite for the conductor. Gifts of other donors, the Crosley Foundation included, assisted in the completion of this key element of the facilities.

In the grand Lobby, the original white marble and red slate flooring has been restored and the white and gold color scheme applied to the cast-iron columns, walls, doors, promenade balcony rail and beamed ceiling, with the coffer soffits in red. Three crystal chandeliers and peripherally placed illuminated globes bring brilliance to the lobby and the commemorative, dedicatory sculpture that has been placed there. The stair lobby and concourse on the northern side has been decorated with a large mirror enhancing the area and adding special reflection. This mirror was presented by the Union Central Life Insurance Company. In the southern concourse a set of convenient escalators moves most of the occupants of the balcony and gallery sections.

High above the main lobby, the original small music hall has been transformed to comfortable modernity and is now designated as "Corbett Tower," a meeting, dining and civic cultural center. The ceiling, which extended to a height of 21 feet to reach above the three windows below the great circular window of the east facade, has been lowered to a more contemporary height, acoustically treated and the walls appointed with burnished gold panels. The carpeted floor is arranged to expose a dance floor in the center area of the room. Crystal chandeliers, hanging below gold ceiling rondelles, and "down" lights offer dramatic effects of light intensities and color tone.

In a complex maze of rods and formed truss members is seen the motorized mechanism for raising and lowering the brilliant central auditorium chandelier.

A bird in song, a sunflower, musical instruments, machinery, plants, architects' tools — The stone carvings shown on these two pages serve to represent the many facets that make Music Hall so special to Cincinnatians.

81

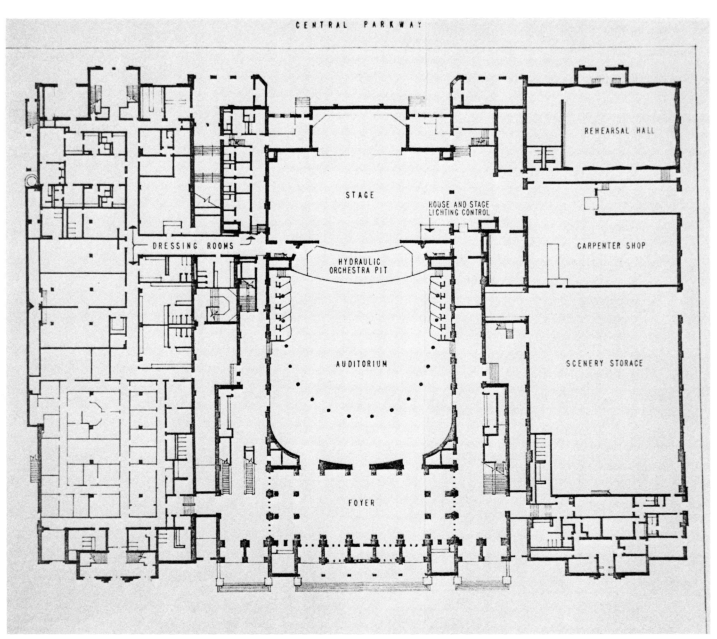

Labels within plan:
REHEARSAL HALL

STAGE

HOUSE AND STAGE
LIGHTING CONTROL

CARPENTER SHOP

DRESSING ROOMS

HYDRAULIC
ORCHESTRA PIT

AUDITORIUM

SCENERY STORAGE

FOYER

This complete first floor plan shows the present design of this entrance level. The newly installed stage equipment, orchestra pit, rehearsal halls and dressing rooms, supporting carpenters' shop, storage areas, etc. assemble in function occupying all of the three originally conceived buildings. The Music Hall Association offices are in the north (right) hall and the Symphony Orchestra administrative offices occupy the front areas of the south building.

The exterior brick and stone surfaces of the three buildings have been cleaned of the soil of many seasons and in the sandblasting and tuck pointing, the patina was removed. The designed complexity of architectural motifs and details has, however, become visible and the sculptural color of the facade ensemble again presented as originally intended by Hannaford when he created his drawings one hundred years ago.

Interesting appointments of symbolic architectural ornaments have appeared. The stone carving of pilaster capitals on the northern building, the "Machinery" Hall, is composed of a pinion wheel and two crossed peen ball hammers nested on fronds of acorn oak. On the southern building, the "Horticulture" Hall, sunflowers are carved in stone inserts in the brick masonry. Over the original coach gates, birds of varied form are the motifs now

clearly visible. The central great facade exhibits numerous stone and cast-iron appointments; the lyre and hunter's horn have been united with the flute and head of the violin in intricate composition. The date stone records 1877 as the birth date of the building. Foliated strap hinges and grills still support the wide, wood entrance doors. High in the east facades of the exposition wings are ornate monograms composed of the letters E and C — perhaps a reference to the early Exposition Commission which was active in the construction program.

This second extensive remodeling and modernization was executed over a period of six years, beginning in 1969 and extending well into 1975. There remain some planned but uncompleted items, the finishing of which, it is hoped, will be possible in the near future.

The president of the Music Hall Association during these busy years was John W. Warrington who, in close collaboration with Roger O. Pellens, manager of Music Hall, and Reuben R. Cohn, city architect, served in administrative offices for the project. The firm of George Schatz and Associates was the designing and supervising architect and engineer; Alan W. Schatz, the project architect, and construction was directed by James

Neumann for the Universal Contracting Corporation of Cincinnati. Landscape planting has been provided by the Federated Garden Clubs of Cincinnati.

Since 1974, the City of Cincinnati, with the aid of the Corbett Foundation, has been developing a new Town Center to the west of Music Hall. A multi-level parking facility has been constructed and a bridge, protected by a plastic translucent vault and served by escalators and stairs, permits pedestrian approach to the southern concourse of the Hall and the remodeled areas of the south pavilion. In architectural relation and south of the festive and uniquely illuminated bridge over Central Parkway, the path of the canal of years past, is the new WCET Crosley Telecommunications Center. This community facility, continuing to grow in the ever-developing field of public educational television, was made possible by grants from the Crosley Foundation, the Jacob G. Schmidlapp Trust, the William H. Albers Foundation, Inc., and many other contributors who gave generously in the building of this two-and-one-half-million-dollar facility. Eventual relation with the Music Hall facilities for the performing arts has been planned and cables are installed in the bridge for this purpose.

As one stands at the heavily designed rail of the balcony over the colorful lobby during the intermission of a concert, watching the promenade below, a sensitive observer may view an interesting, quiet but very pleasant element of the scene.

Above the crowd, on high plinths, stand the stately bronze and marble portrait sculptures of those honored for their contributions to the cultural life that has found stage in this unique environment. Here, also, are the cast panels commemorating outstanding events in the musical history of the great hall. No description of the architecture of this lobby or of this Music Hall is complete if the gallery of artists and philanthropists remains unrecognized. Here is the figure of Reuben Springer, placed on a high granite base, the 1882 work of Preston Powers. Here, also, is the bronze figure of the beloved maestro and chorus master, Theodore Thomas, along with those of Stephen Collins Foster, composer; Max Rudolph, conductor; J. Ralph Corbett, philanthropist.

At the southern end of this illustrious line is a high, finely finished marble figure, bearded and draped as a noble Roman. By careful inspection, one may find the single name AIKEN, and in that name is reflected a significant Cincinnati spirit. As the first superintendent of music in the public schools, Charles Aiken in 1876 engendered the realization by his pupils of the need that all have for the joys of music. Together, they presented three thousand 19th century dollars as the schoolchildren's contribution to the building of Cincinnati's Music Hall.

In a review of the architectural planning of Music Hall, the description of a pipe organ may seem misplaced. In this structure, however, a great organ was a necessary element of the architectural plan as a result of the public interest in such an instrument to support renditions of oratorios and choral concerts. A large sum of money was raised to purchase a fine, fully equipped, wide-range organ, centrally placed in the area designated for the large choruses. Designed and built by the firm of Hook and Hastings of Boston, the great assembly of pipes and wood structure rose 65 feet from the stage level to the top of the highest pipe, which was 32 feet in length. The smallest

pipe was a tiny metal whistle. The encased organ measured 50 feet in width by 15 feet in depth, and in position it served effectively to divide the choral seating arrangement. A vastly complicated musical instrument, the organ had a total of 81 stops and 6277 pipes and, within, a carillon of 30 notes. An "echo" organ was installed above the auditorium ceiling directly over the central mural. The instrument was activated by five bellows worked by five hydraulic motors placed in the basement below the stage and fed by a six-inch main from the city's Mt. Auburn reservoir.

The entire assembly, except the "echo" instrument, was completed and played in that initial musical festival of 1878.

Robert Rogers was the designer of the organ case-work which was constructed of wild cherry. The numerous enclosing panels received carved wood embellishments. The carving, begun in September of 1878, included floral and allegorical subjects. The names of the composers Bach, Beethoven and Handel in a key central position were crowned with laurel, while Mozart and Mendelssohn surmounted panels of trumpetvine and the passion flower. Twelve other composers were similarly honored. Symbolic presentations of Even, Noon and Morning and the four seasons were included. Much of this was the handiwork of the "Cincinnati ladies, volunteers in aid — in the finishing and adding beautiful touches to the Music Hall and its organ." In a competition open only to the ladies, ten were chosen to do the work under the direction of Mr. Benjamin Pitman. With similar verve, the superintendent of the McMicken School of Design, W. H. Humphreys, ornamented the visible pipes of the organ in silver and gold, with arabesque bands and borders.

Today, one hundred years later, the organ has been dismembered, sections of it given or sold to churches and institutions scattered over a wide region. All but two carved panels have been saved and installed on the auditorium bulkhead of the stage as a memorial facia. Unfortunately, this frieze is often concealed from view by the movable stage floor extensions and by the orchestra when playing in the pit. Several deeply carved panels of floral composition, having been retained in storage by the city, have been placed in the collections of the Cincinnati Historical Society. The largest, a horizontal, central motif of the facade of the organ case is assumed to be the work of Henry Fry and his son William, both of whom were instructors in wood carving at the McMicken School of Design. The older Fry, of Bath, England, had worked on screens in Westminster Abbey and in the Houses of Parliament under Charles Barry and Augustus Pugin, both strongly influential to the taste of this High Victorian art period.

A new organ has been provided by Cincinnati's philanthropists, the Corbett Foundation. Designed and fabricated by the Baldwin Piano and Organ Company, it was donated to the City of Cincinnati in 1974 by Mr. and Mrs. J. Ralph Corbett, with the counsel of the late Maestro Thomas Schippers, who directed its first use in a concert on October 11, 1974, presenting, as organist and conductor, the Poulenc Organ Concerto.

This remarkable instrument, known as Opus XV, is a multiwave-form organ with electro-acoustic pipes arranged in two movable platforms, each 15 feet high and 10 feet wide. The distribution of tonal sources around the entire proscenium arch provides a very spacious effect for the organ, supplementing the orchestra sound radiating from the orchestra shell. The superior acoustics of the hall complement the organ and vice versa, the entire movable instrument, console and pipes are stored in the stage areas when not in use.

Designers of this great organ were Daniel C. Martin, scientist-acoustical engineer, and Edward M. Jones, electronic engineer, both of Cincinnati. This organ, the result of many years of research and development, combining computer techniques, optics, electronics, solid-stage physics, dynamics and photography, is truly a symbol of the inevitable change that has been accommodated in this Music Hall through one hundred years of service.

A view of the complicated suspension system of stage equipment, set between and into the roof trusses.

A secondary or "echo" organ enclosure remains to be seen in the roof space, located directly above the auditorium ceiling mural with the chandelier suspension passing through.

Nineteenth-century organ pipes and shutters are still to be seen above the auditorium ceiling. This is the "secondary" organ, the sound passing through a metal ceiling grill in a swirl pattern.

The west facade of Music Hall as seen through the recently constructed plastic covered bridge and gazebo of the Town Center.

The covered bridge over Central Parkway to the parking decks of the Town Center. The Crosley Telecommunications Center is seen through the planting.

The north pavilion in the foreground contained the early "Power" or "Machinery" Hall. The distant southern unit was originally to house the horticulture displays. Music Hall in the center marked by the sharply conicle, flanking towers, perhaps at no time included the pinnacle ornament or great figure which was shown on the architect's design.

The west facade as seen from the bridge approach. Plum Street and the Miami-Erie Canal have been replaced by the Central Parkway. Minor changes in the lower zones of the buildings were made, but the original mass remains unaltered.

SECTION THREE
ON STAGE

The following photographic collection is not meant to be all-encompassing but rather to capture briefly some of the events and performers, both on stage and backstage, who have made Music Hall come alive in recent years.

Arthur Fiedler

"On the occasions when I have conducted the Cincinnati Symphony in the Music Hall (which is quite a few times) I have always been struck by the lovely acoustics of that old hall. I think that it is wonderful that the people of Cincinnati had such good foresight to leave the Hall as it was originally built (with the exception of the backstage, dressing rooms, etc.). I think that it compares favorably with the best halls in the United States. It should be good for another 100 years. I always look forward to my appearances there."

Beverly Sills sings the role of Queen Elizabeth I in "Roberto Devereux" in 1974.

The lyric beauty of Luciano Pavarotti's voice filled Music Hall for the first time on February 27, 1978, and the audience that heard this "voice among voices" was hypnotized by the power of the world-famous Italian tenor. He has been described as the equivalent of a Horowitz on the piano; a Casals on the cello; a Heifetz on the violin.

Mary Costa stars in a 1974 production of "La Perichole."

Artur Rubinstein

"Time and space do not permit me to adequately express my recollections of the many performances I have given in Cincinnati's Music Hall, but I can say that this building is one of the first in America actually built for music."

Mice wait in the wings for their entrance in Act I of the 1977 "Nutcracker."

For more than fifty years, 85-year-old Andres Segovia has been thrilling music lovers and classical guitar enthusiasts. The resurgence of popularity of the instrument in the 20th century is attributed to this "poet of the guitar."

As the camera saw it — the Cincinnati Symphony in a live TV broadcast with Erich Kunzel conducting.

The witch (Robert Schmorr) captures Hansel and Gretel (Eileen Shelle (l.) and Susanne Marsee(r.)) in the 1973 production.

"The Merry Widow" (Karan Armstrong) makes her first entrance and all the eligible gentlemen vie for her favor in the 1975 production.

Arthur Fiedler, whose Boston Pops concerts have made him a popular figure, makes an entrance for a 1975 concert of the Cincinnati Symphony Orchestra.

Melissa Hale appears as the Sugar Plum Fairy and John Ashton as the Cavalier in the 1977 production of "Nutcracker."

Beverly Sills

"In the early days of my career, I remember with great affection the days and nights in the Zoo singing opera. One night the animals were so restless the cast printed a little sign with the words 'La Traviata starring Beverly Seals.' I also remember with great horror the nights during 'Tales of Hoffman', I think it was, when the temperature never dropped below 90°. So, the move to Music Hall was, at first, one that would simply make my life more comfortable. The first time I sang in it was a revelation of interior beauty and acoustical delight. I well recall singing 'Cleopatra' to the late, great Norman Treigle's Caesar and thinking 'What a perfect setting.' I have always said that Art is the signature of a civilization. Cincinnatians have signed their names large and clear."

When Thomas Schippers became music director of the Cincinnati Symphony Orchestra in 1970, he described himself as a "plant in the desert that needs twenty years to flower." He never had that chance to mature. His long struggle with lung cancer ended with his death in December, 1977, at the age of forty-seven. Thomas Schippers was one of the most accomplished conductors of the era, and his years with the Cincinnati Symphony Orchestra will be remembered as special ones in CSO history. But perhaps his greatest legacy is the bequest of the bulk of his almost one-million-dollar estate to the Orchestra he loved. "Cincinnatians have inherited from Maestro Schipper's parting gesture," said a Cincinnati Enquirer *editorial, "a continuing challenge to preserve the tradition that his life and career helped to shape."*

In this series of photographs, Schippers conducts Beethoven's Ninth Symphony at the 1976 May Festival. In October, 1976, he made his last appearance with the Cincinnati Symphony Orchestra.

103

Tara Moore appears as Clara in the 1977 "Nutcracker."

When Schippers fell ill, David Stahl was among those called in to take his place as conductor of the Cincinnati Symphony.

Operatic opulence at its finest — the coronation scene from "Boris Godunov" in the 1974 summer season, with Norman Treigle singing the title role.

Dorothy Kirsten sings the title role in "Tosca" in 1976 with Cincinnati-trained John Alexander as Mario Cavatadossi.

Erich Kunzel's view of his role as a conductor is to entertain, and every year he fills Music Hall with capacity crowds for the immensely popular Eight O'Clock Concert Series. In September, 1977, he was named director of the newly created Cincinnati Pops Orchestra.

Max Rudolf

"Ten years ago George Szell came from his home base, Cleveland's famed Severance Hall, to conduct the Cincinnati Symphony Orchestra. After his concert he told me: 'I envy you your hall'. He was not the first, nor the last, guest conductor to enjoy Music Hall's exceptionally fine acoustics, spacious structure, and old-world atmosphere. It was my good fortune to call Music Hall my musical home for twelve years and I cherish the memories of nearly five hundred concerts on its' stage, an experience shared with the world's great soloists, a distinguished group of musicians in the Orchestra, and an understanding, faithful audience. My warmest wishes go to Music Hall on its' 100th anniversary and to Cincinnati's citizens who have supported it so splendidly."

Cincinnati-born James Levine conducts the audience in singing "The Star-Spangled Banner."

Complete with an elephant from the Zoo, the triumphal procession wends onstage during a 1976 production of "Aida."

Katherine Turner, Karen Karibo and Pam Willingham in "Ah! May the Red Rose Live Always" from the 1977 presentation of "Dear Friends and Gentle Hearts."

The end nears for Patricia Craig as Mimi in "La Bohome." Around her bed in the 1974 production are, from left, Joseph Galiano as Schaunard, Barbara Daniels as Musetta, Raymond Gibbs as Rodolfo, Thomas McKinney as Marcello and Tom Fox as Colline.

Plants and flowers deck the foyer statue of Theodore Thomas, the May Festival's first conductor.

An alumnus of the former Cincinnati Conservatory of Music, John Alexander returns to Cincinnati as Roberto in a 1974 presentation of "Roberto Devereux."

Months of training behind them, chorus and orchestra open the May Festival performance of "Gurre Lieder" in 1975.

"Carmen" nears its violent end in a 1976 production with Beverly Wollf as Carmen and Harry Theyard as Don Jose.

Julius Rudel

"In these days of super acousticians and engineered relay systems, it is the supreme pleasure to perform in an old hall where so much glorious sound comes naturally. And how few places there are in the world where opera and symphony are equally at home in such beautiful surroundings."

Donna Grisez dances in the premiere of "Grande Tarantella"
in December, 1977.

Comfort's the rule at performances of Opera.

Conductor Carmen DeLeone, shows youngsters at a Lollipop Concert a strange way of making music.

In silhouette against the audience, Alan Titus sings in Bernstein's "Mass" in the May Festival of 1972.

Eileen Farrell

"For a long time I felt almost like a native of Cincinnati. I was flattered beyond words to have been invited to sing in your wonderful musical community so, so often. May the second one hundred years be even greater than the first."

*A Cincinnati Opera favorite, Norman Treigle appears as
Boris in a 1974 production of "Boris Godunov."*

Maestro Thomas Schippers leads Gina Bachauer forward to receive her applause after a concert in 1976.

James McCracken appears as Manrico in "Il Trovatore" in 1975.

These children are nervously awaiting the one-hour-away start of "Nutcracker."

Rene Hallman and John Nelson perform in "Nutcracker."

Julian Patrick sings the role of Paquillo in the 1974 production of "La Perichole."

Alan Titus

"There are occasions in a singer's life where the time, place, music and audience are so 'right' that by some unknown force all become one and that incredible magic of the theater happens. The performances of Leonard Bernstein's 'Mass' I did in the Music Hall was one of those wonderful moments where all elements worked together in such harmony that those evenings remain one of the most exciting experiences I've ever had on stage."

CSO concertmaster Phillip Ruder rehearses "Capriccio No. 2" for violin and orchestra which the composer, Krzysztof Penderecki, conducted in a 1977 concert.

Barbara Karp, first woman to direct an opera in Cincinnati, and Production Manager Tom Connell making sure all's ready for the curtain at a performance of "The Ballad of Baby Doe" in 1976.

Renata Scotto as Norma and Joann Grillo as Adalgisa in a duet in Act II of "Norma" in the summer of 1977.

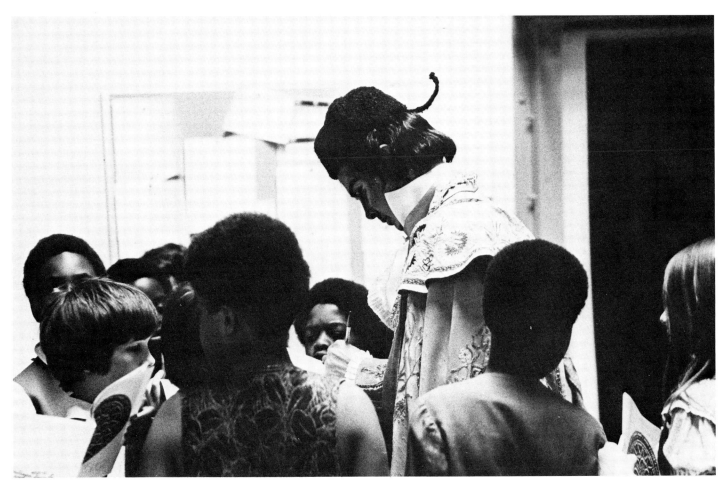

*Alfred Anderson, singing the role of Escamillo in a 1976
Summer Opera production of ''Carmen,'' signs autographs
for youngsters in the childrens' chorus.*

*James Morris as Mephistopheles and Kenneth Riegel as
Faust in a centerstage duet in a 1975 production, with Linda
Cook in the background.*

Mstislav Rostropovich

"I believe the Music Hall is truly one of the great concert halls in America. I have always looked forward to appearing there and I want to congratulate everyone associated with it in the celebration of its 100th anniversary."

*Performers are not only people. Two horses await their cues in
the scene shop during an Opera performance of "Carmen" in
1976.*

*Martina Arroyo as Aida and James King as Radames appear
in a 1973 Opera performance of "Aida."*

Roberta Peters

"For a concert artist who performs in many different halls both at home and abroad there have to be some favorites. The Cincinnati Music Hall is certainly one of my favorites, for both concerts and opera. The acoustics and the audience of the Hall always make for a pleasurable experience for me."

Maestro Leonard Slatkin directs the Symphony in concert
October 8, 1977.

Aida (Martina Arroyo) joins Radames (James King) in the crypt where he awaits his execution in Act IV of "Aida" in the 1974 Opera production.

Aaron Copland

"Cincinnati is lucky to have had so fine a Music Hall for the past century. I shall always have a vivid memory of my concert there with the Cincinnati Symphony. It was a pleasure to work with them, and to give a concert in a hall that does full justice to the sound of that fine Orchestra."

James Levine

"Cincinnati is fortunate to have one of the very greatest concert halls in the world in its' beloved Music Hall. The Hall has special meaning for me, having heard most of my first performances of the symphonic repertoire there when I was growing up in Cincinnati. And then during my years as May Festival Music Director, it was the scene of the first performances I conducted anywhere of such works as Mahler's Eighth Symphony, Haydn's 'Creation' and Wagner's 'Lohengrin'. The only venerable halls in America that compare with Music Hall in acoustical quality are Boston's Symphony Hall and New York's Carnegie Hall—a most select company indeed."

Two fascinated youngsters watch from the wings at a "Lollipop Concert," one of many staged by the Symphony to introduce children to fine music and the instruments that produce it.

PUBLISHER'S NOTE

Luke Feck, in his Introduction, praised Cincinnati's tradition of citizen commitment and participation. In our opinion, one of the best examples of this tradition is the publication of this book. Rarely do publishers receive a manuscript assembled by committee, but in the case of *Cincinnati's Music Hall,* the project was the work of a unique group of people. The following is a listing of the committee members. We wish to acknowledge their outstanding accomplishments and to thank them for their efforts.

Charles Westheimer, chairman of the Music Hall Centennial Committee, approached us with the idea for the book.

Mary A. Heller, chairman of the Landmarks subcommittee, and Martha A. Lang, committee member, spearheaded the project and saw it to completion. Enough cannot be said about the amount of dedication and work these two ladies contributed to this book. The Miami Purchase Association for Historic Preservation and The Cincinnati Enquirer, their respective employers, must also be recognized for their unusual support and contributions to this project.

Other members of the Landmarks subcommittee who helped develop the concept of the book were John Duteil, Carolyn Lea Mond, Robert W. Rodger, and Sister Rosine.

Mrs. Fred Lazarus, III must also be thanked for her help in obtaining the comments from the artists whose photographs appear in the On Stage section of the book.

Dr. Zane L. Miller wishes to acknowledge the assistance, intellectual stimulation, and counsel of the following persons in the preparation of his manuscript.

Professor Henry D. Shapiro of the University of Cincinnati Department of History; Allen I. Marcus, graduate teaching assistant, and the other students and participants in the Laboratory in American Civilization, Department of History, U. C. Education Council; Robert Fairbanks, graduate student in the history at U. C.; Laura Chace and Frances Forman of the Cincinnati Historical Society, who also assisted George Roth in the research for his architectural study; and Alice Vestal and Ann Van Camp of the Department of Special Collections and the Archival Collections of the University of Cincinnati.

George F. Roth was aided by the following persons in the preparation of his essay on the construction of Music Hall:

Alan W. Schatz, architect, who furnished architectural drawings and details of construction; Thomas Landise of Cincinnati and New Jersey, architect, who preserved Hannaford's early and later drawings and placed them in the files of the Historical Society; Roger O. Pellens, David P. Curry and Roy F. Hopper of the Music Hall Association; Dr. Daniel C. Martin, Baldwin Organ Company, co-designer of the Opus XV organ; Charles Vaughn, manager, WCET-TV; Mrs. Grace Keam of the Cincinnati Art Museum library staff; Miss Dorothea Bauer of the Crosely Foundation; Mrs. Karl Schlachter, whose collection of publications of Cincinnati's early events and people was invaluable in the research; and the Corbett Foundation, for the well-written documenting of facts in its Twenty-Year Report, 1955-1975.

The editorial work of Ellis Rawnsley of *The Cincinnati Enquirer* and Reba Karp of our staff, must also be acknowledged with grateful appreciation.

Jordan & Company, Publishers
Virginia Beach, Virginia

FOOTNOTES

THE HISTORY

[1] Robert G. Albion, *The Rise of New York Port* (N. Y.: Scribner's, 1939), is the classic study of New York's rise to the top of the urban hierarchy, but we lack a solid and comprehensive account of its relative decline during the mid-19th century. On this point, however, see David R. Goldfield, "Pursuing the American Dream: Cities in the Old South," in Blaine A. Brownell and David R. Goldfield, eds., *The City in Southern History* (Port Washington, N. Y.: Kennikat Press, 1977), pp. 52-91, and Michael P. Conzen, "The Maturing Urban System in the United States, 1840-1910," *Annals of the Association of American Geographers,* Vol. 67, No. 1 (March, 1977), pp. 88-108. The other "reserve" cities were Boston, Philadelphia, Providence and Baltimore, and an amendement to the act added to the list Washington, Albany, Pittsburgh, Cleveland, Detroit, Milwaukee, Louisville, Leavenworth, and San Francisco.

[2] See Charles N. Glaab and A. Theodore Brown, *A History of Urban America* (N. Y.: The Macmillan Company, 1967), pp. 73-81, for predictions that one or another city of the interior would outstrip the eastern seaboard cities and become the metropolis of America.

[3] Zane L. Miller, "Cincinnati: A Bicentennial Assessment," *The Cincinnati Historical Society Bulletin,* Vol. 34, No. 4 (Winter, 1976), pp. 239-240. For two interesting recent works dealing in rather different ways, both from each other and this essay, with urbanization and the arts see Helen Lefkowitz Horovitz, *Culture & The City: Cultural Philanthropy in Chicago from the 1880's to 1917* (Lexington: The University Press of Kentucky, 1976), and Richard Sennett, *The Fall of Public Man* (N. Y.: Alfred A. Knopf, 1977).

[4] Louise R. Thomas, *A History of the Cincinnati Symphony Orchestra to 1931* (Cincinnati: unpublished Ph.D. dissertation, University of Cincinnati, 1972), Vol. I, pp. 20-28, 39-43.

[5] *Ibid.,* pp. 20-21. Also see Cincinnati Music Hall Association, *Golden Jubilee. . ., op. cit.,* pp. 20-21, in a resolution protesting the Mayor's stance which the Association sent to City Council. On the zoo issue see Judith Spraul-Schmidt, *The Late Nineteenth Century City and Its Cultural Institutions: The Cincinnati Zoological Garden, 1873-1898* (Cincinnati: unpublished M. A. thesis, University of Cincinnati, 1977), pp. 26-27.

[6] Thomas, *op. cit.,* pp. 258-260, 269-276, 280-293, 298-306. The use of Music Hall by the Symphony Orchestra to 1931 can be traced in Thomas, *op. cit.,* Vol. II, and thereafter in the annual reports of the Cincinnati Music Hall Association.

[7] The best account of politics and government in Cincinnati during the 1920's is William A. Baughin, *Murray Seasongood: Twentieth Century Urban Reformer* (Cincinnati: unpublished Ph.D. dissertation, University of Cincinnati, 1972.)

[8] On the "community of limited liability" see Morris Janowitz, *The Community Press in an Urban Setting: The Social Elements of Urbanism* (Chicago: The University of Chicago Press, second edition, 1967 [first edition, 1952]), pp. 210-213. The Master Plan quotes are from Cincinnati City Planning Commission, *The Cincinnati Metropolitan Master Plan and the Official City Plan of the City of Cincinnati,* (Cincinnati: The Cincinnati City Planning Commission, [1948]), pp. 7-10.

THE ARCHITECTURE

American Architect and Building News, 1876, 1877, 1878
The Architectural Record, 1908
Archives of the Cincinnati Historical Society

Archives of Timothy C. Day Library, Ohio Mechanics Institute and Ohio College of Applied Science; University of Cincinnati

Journal of the Society of Architectural Historians.

Library of the Cincinnati Art Museum.

Publication of Cincinnati Music Hall Association, Golden Jubilee, Cincinnati Music Hall, 1878-1929

Records of the Cincinnati Chapter, American Institute of Architects.